JULES VERNE

AND HIS WORK

I. O. EVANS
F.R.G.S.

JULES VERNE

AND HIS WORK

TWAYNE PUBLISHERS, INC.

Manufactured in the
United States of America

CONTENTS

ILLUSTRATIONS

PREFACE

UNTIL recently Jules Verne was remembered only for a handful of his most popular books, and especially those 'adapted' for the screen. He has long been renowned as the virtual founder of science fiction and as the author of some other exciting adventure stories, but how many of his admirers realize that he also wrote historical stories, love stories, detective stories, works of social criticism and a revival in scientific terms of the traditional 'Gothic story'—to say nothing of an exhaustive history of exploration?

For some years, however, interest in his works has been reviving. In America several have appeared as paperbacks. In France a number have been produced, gorgeously illustrated in colour, some impressively—and expensively—intended for adults, some abridged—and cheaper—for youth. In Britain a new edition of his works is in progress; already over forty have been published in cloth binding and some are now appearing as paperbacks.

This re-awakening of interest is partly due to the spectacular films more or less based on his stories, and partly to our realization, in these days of space-flight, that we ourselves are living in a Vernian and Wellsian world. But surely it also indicates that the reading public, surfeited with mass-produced thrillers and westerns and 'space opera', with 'debunking' biographies, with 'sick' humour, the 'anti-hero', and the 'kitchen sink', are returning with relief to what is traditionally one of the great themes of literature, the story of strong, adventurous, and self-disciplined heroes and heroines, displaying dogged determination and stalwart courage in facing hardship and peril for the sake of a worthy ideal.

Verne's work is not only being read, it is now being treated as a serious contribution to literature. It is being subjected to penetrating criticism, attempts being made to trace influences and origins and bringing unsuspected facts to light. It has, too, been exposed to a sort of psycho-analytical treatment, with the usual startling, though sometimes unconvincing, results. Remarkable efforts, which would appeal to Baconians, have been made to trace cryptic significance in some of its minor features, one result being to confirm that the books which bear his name were actually written by Jules Verne.

My own aim is more modest, to give a comprehensive account of his work, discussing his life simply in so far as this throws light upon it, for I agree with his own view that a writer interests his public only as a writer. I cannot help feeling, moreover, that a writer's personal affairs are his own business and no one else's.

Without, save exceptionally, spoiling the 'surprise endings' in which he delighted, by revealing them prematurely, I seek to discuss his stories just sufficiently to enable the reader to decide which of them he is likely to enjoy, and to warn him off those which might disappoint him, for it cannot be denied that Verne over-wrote himself and produced some inferior stuff. I have tried to make the treatment I give each book roughly in proportion to its merits; where I deal with it at length the reader might wish to read it for himself, but where I dismiss it in a few sentences, he might, with a few exceptions, prefer to do the same.

My material is chiefly drawn from the standard biographies by Kenneth Allott and Verne's niece, Mme Allotte de la Fuÿe, supplemented by the other sources included in the bibliography. Certain contradictions in these suggest that when it came to details some of the authors were drawing on their imagination, just as the summaries they give of Verne's works suggest that they were at times relying on a somewhat unreliable memory.

Finally, I hope that I have succeeded in doing justice to the literary gifts of Jules Verne, to his unflagging industry, his versatility, his descriptive powers, his imagination bounded only by his love of accuracy, and, above all, to the lofty moral idealism which always inspired his work.

He might well have re-echoed the sentences in which his publisher summed up his own career. In these Hetzel declared that he had reached, without regret, the end of a life which could no longer be useful. . . . He had left behind him a library which his country—we might well say mankind—needed; he had given all his strength to this, and he never regretted it.

I. O. E.

INTRODUCTION

ON THE TRAIL OF JULES VERNE

'IS THAT the I. O. Evans who sent us a manuscript on H. G. Wells?' asked an unfamiliar voice on the telephone. 'Yes? I'm speaking for Sidgwick and Jackson, publishers. We are not interested in your Wells MS, but there is something else we should like to discuss with you. Could we meet sometime?'

We arranged time and place. 'But what is it you want to talk about?' I enquired.

'I'll tell you that when we meet' was the cryptic reply, and then the caller rang off.

A little perplexed, I kept the appointment. After the usual generalities, I was asked what I thought the prospects would be for a new edition of the short stories of H. G. Wells.

'Not practical,' I replied. 'They've been done time and again. Besides, there'd be the question of copyright.'

'Well, what about a volume of short stories by Jules Verne?'

'A very good idea,' I said epigrammatically, 'except that Jules Verne didn't write short stories!'

(This, I learned later, was not strictly true; Verne had in fact written several short stories. But for all practical purposes it was true enough, for these were then mostly unobtainable, and anyhow they are inferior to his longer works.)

After further discussion we hit on a practicable scheme, to quote the most exciting passages from his science fiction stories, with brief notes explaining what led up to the episodes and what followed them.

This idea fascinated me, for I had long been enthusiastic for Jules Verne. During my childhood the only library within reach was that of our Church Sunday School, from which its members could borrow two volumes a week, 'one sacred and one secular'. The reader can guess which we chose! Most of the library's fiction was of the rather goody-goody *Eric or Little by Little* type, but there was one volume which seemed to have got in by accident, Verne's *Journey to the Centre of the Earth.*

An avid bookworm, I borrowed it whenever it was available, read and re-read it, and almost got it by heart. Years later, when I began to study geology, I found its technical terms not forbidding but evocative; they were the sort of thing I'd seen in Verne. Indeed, it was through reading this book that I became a 'popularizer' of geology, an amateur speleologist, and a life-long science fiction addict.

Whenever I wanted to 'brush up my French' the obvious thing was to read Verne in the original, and from my first visit to Paris I returned in triumph with a paperback edition of *Voyage à la Centre de la Terre*.

So I felt qualified to compile the volume the firm had in mind, and the question next arose whether I could write acceptably. They settled this tactfully by the simple plan of asking me to review one of their latest books for their house magazine. Then it was decided to push ahead.

Now came an unexpected difficulty. Most of the public libraries limited their stocks of Verne to a few of his best-known books, and as I wanted to quote from some of the others it looked as if I would have to spend many a Saturday afternoon—I was then a Civil Servant—in the British Museum Reading Room, copying long sections by hand and typing them out later.

Then I learned that the Verne collection is centralized in the Public Library at Wandsworth, where the Borough Librarian, Mr Edmund V. Corbett, was most sympathetic, letting me borrow all I needed. For *Sphinx of the Ice-fields*, however, even his collection failed me, and that did involve copying out a section in the British Museum.

The anthology, *Jules Verne: Master of Science Fiction* (now out of print) received quite a good press and a few years ago it had unexpected repercussions. Again a publisher approached me, this time by letter addressed to 'I. O. Jones'.

Mr Bernard Hanison, intending to publish a new edition of Verne, had enquired at Wandsworth Library about a likely editor; Mr Corbett had been good enough to suggest me, and again put his collection at my disposal. What was needed was not a new translation but a revisal of the books already in existence.

First we had to settle what Mr Hanison wanted, an 'authoritative' edition including all that Verne wrote, or an abridged one adapted for a modern public and omitting the technical detail with which that enthusiastic armchair geographer Jules Verne delighted to encumber his narratives. As what was needed was something that people would read, we decided to leave out the detail—very wisely, for surely no author more repaid judicious skipping.

We naturally expected the task to be fairly simple, needing only omissions and correction of printer's errors and so forth. I soon learned our mistake: many of the existing versions—by no means all—were in such stilted language that they had to be largely re-written. There were occasional gross errors in translation, and sometimes the translator had got so bogged down in the technical detail that it was impossible to see what he meant.

As the work proceeded my ambitions began to soar. Finding that many of Verne's later stories had never appeared in Britain, I wondered whether they were worth translating. They were—indeed, some of them were among the best he wrote. The difficulty was to get hold of the originals, for almost all were so scarce they were not even in the British Museum.

Here I received invaluable help from the late S. André Peyre, a French *litterateur* and a Jules Verne enthusiast. Not only did he lend me several of these inaccessible works, he helped me with the queries that cropped up during the task.

Other scarce Verne's had to be hunted for in the bookshops during my visits to France, and in one I found half-a-dozen 'remaindered'—and as yet untranslated. Sending the others on by post, I kept one for which I had a special use.

When at the Customs I was asked if I had anything to declare, I looked as furtive as I could, leaned forward and muttered confidentially that I had bought one book—'the sort of thing one can't get in England'.

The Customs Officer glared at me suspiciously and demanded to see it. But he relaxed and smiled as he waved me on when he saw the jacket. It displayed a three-master, a giant octopus, and a scared-looking seaman. And its title and author? *Le Serpent de Mer* by Jules Verne!

Most of the bookshops were unable to help, but occasionally I came across what in the circumstances it seems appropriate to call a *trouvaille*. On a visit to Tours I found that the town boasted four shops specializing in old books. The first three were so unhelpful it hardly seemed worth while going to the other, only a stone's throw from the hotel where I was staying. But it proved to contain two books I especially sought, the elusive volume *Le Sphinx des Glaces*, which I wanted for the British Museum; and the collection of short stories, *Hier et Demain*, practically unobtainable and containing what is believed to be the very last narrative that Jules Verne ever wrote, which I wanted to translate.

In Le Pouligen, a small Breton fishing-port, the French equivalent of a 'twopenny lending library' included another unobtainable Verne, *L'Agence Thompson and Co.* This consisted of two battered paper-back volumes, soiled and almost falling to pieces. I wanted to purchase them but the librarian was doubtful; the books, she reminded me, were there to lend, not to sell.

In the most eloquent French I could muster, I explained my ambition, to make the works of a great French literary man available to the British public, and she looked impressed. I also asked her when this book had last been borrowed and she had to admit that it had never been asked for yet.

When she objected, as was obvious, that the book was in singularly bad condition, I explained that for my purposes that did not matter; and when she pointed out that it might be defective, I said I would take my chance on that. Finally she protested that she would not know what to charge me, but at last we agreed on a price. She was kind enough to pack the books for sending by post and again I mustered all my French to thank her as profusely as I could, short of kissing her hand.

New translations apart, there were two books which specially appealed to me. I was anxious to combine in one volume abridgments of Verne's *Le Sphinx des Glaces* with the incomplete work of Edgar Allan Poe to which it forms a sequel, *The Narrative of Arthur Gordon Pym*. Here I was fortunate enough to have the co-operation of Mr Basil Ashmore, as great an enthusiast for Poe as I am for Verne. The English translation of the former book, for some reason entitled *An Antarctic Mystery*, was as unobtainable as ever, but Mr Ashmore was able to supply the volume of the *Boy's Own Paper* in which it had been serialized.

Journey to the Centre of the Earth, I suggested, with the publishers' approval, deserved, as a classic of science fiction, to be newly translated. In this task, I thought, some knowledge of geology would be useful, and it was.

The other books I suggested for the new edition were naturally those that I thought most deserved inclusion. When we get far enough down the list to arrive at Verne's less successful works we can decide whether they are worth re-publishing.

So much interest did the edition arouse that the publishers shared my view that the time was ripe for a newly-compiled biography of Jules Verne: Kenneth Allott's excellent critique was published as long ago as 1940, and the more recent French books deal only with special aspects of Verne's work.

The task involved making visits to the Municipal Libraries at Nantes and Amiens. At Amiens, where the 'Verniana' is centralized, the library staff were especially helpful, co-operating with my efforts to work at full pressure all the time the library was open, and seemingly mildly surprised that I should insist on breaking off for ten minutes during the afternoon for the 'le four o'clock'.

While in Amiens I stayed in a small hotel next door to Verne's old home on what is now the Boulevard Jules Verne. Its present occupants, a leading oil-firm, were very courteous, allowing me to visit the room where he worked and to ascend the tower which dominates the house, and leaving me alone for a few minutes 'meditation'. Needless to say, I paid a special visit to the Amiens Cemetery where a monument represents Jules Verne as rising from death 'onward to immortality and eternal youth'—or, as I am tempted to suspect, bursting indignantly from the tomb to denounce Hollywood for vulgarizing his themes.

Finally, it is my pleasant duty to acknowledge the help which I have received from sources too numerous to mention: the name 'Jules Verne' seems to work like a charm in evoking sympathy and help. From various Embassies, notably the Icelandic, and from such bodies as the Aerodynamical Division of the National Physical Laboratory and the Royal Geographical Society I received willing co-operation.

The libraries which have been helpful include those of the British Museum and of Wandsworth; with those of Amiens and Nantes which brought to my notice material hitherto unknown in Britain. Nor must I forget my publishers, first Mr Bernard Hanison and then Arco Publications, who gave me encouragement and a free hand in compiling the edition; nor my friend and former colleague Mr Bernard Newman for helpful criticism and advice.

JULES VERNE

AND HIS WORK

I

Running away from Home

MANY boys have thought of 'running away to sea'. Many young intellectuals have thought of refusing well-paid work for the doubtful chances of a literary career. Few have actually done either. Jules Verne did both.

The son of Pierre Verne, 'a lawyer with the soul of a classical poet', and of Sophie, *née* Allotte de la Fuÿe, he was born on 8 February 1828, in a corner house at the end of the Rue Kervegan on what was then the Ile Feydeau, separated by two arms of the River Loire from the rest of Nantes.

There is no longer an Ile Feydeau; the narrower channel has been filled in and the former island merged into the northern part of Nantes. Verne's birthplace is still there, with a plaque on its walls to announce that 'Jules Verne, *Romancier, Précurseur,* was born in this house', but it has an air of having seen better days. Built in the rather forbidding style of French urban architecture, its wall rises several stories high from the pavement, broken only by the windows and the shutters which flank them: though a dwelling-house it might just as well be an institution or a factory, and there is nothing about it to suggest romance.

At the beginning of the last century, however, the Ile Feydeau was picturesque enough to inspire a sketch by Turner and to fill young Verne with thoughts of romance. About thirty miles from the mouth of the Loire, it was certainly an exciting place for a small boy to live in. As he wandered about its quays, little Jules could feast his eyes on a wide variety of wares—shell-fish, exotic fruits and nuts, parrots and monkeys in their cages; he could hear unfamiliar accents and smell exciting odours. He could watch the ships putting out or coming in, not only the local fishing craft but the great ocean-going vessels with their towering masts.

During the spring floods, when the swollen waters of the Loire came surging past, Jules could easily imagine that he was actually aboard a ship. He could even fancy, with mingled alarm and expectation, that the small island had been torn bodily away from its foundations and was being swept out to sea.

Indoors he could revel in tales of adventure, for first he had read to him, and then he learned to read for himself, translations of Fenimore Cooper and Walter Scott and 'the Robinsons', not only *Robinson Crusoe* but *The Swiss Family Robinson*, which he thought the better of the two.

One of his uncles had exciting tales to tell him of a relative, Chateaubriand, who had travelled into the Far West among the Red Indians. The English might claim to have discovered the North-west Passage, his uncle assured him, but it was really a Frenchman who had done so, not merely a fellow-countryman but a distant kinsman of Jules Verne himself!

The dame-school which Jules attended brought further thoughts of adventure. Its teacher, Mme Samblain, never tired of telling her pupils how her husband, a ship's captain, had had to leave her to go to sea almost while they were on their honeymoon. Though that had been thirty years before and nothing had since been heard of him, she was still confident that one day he would come back.

'Children,' Verne said later in life, 'be glad you didn't work too hard at school. Studious children invariably turn into stupid youths and half-witted grown-ups.'[1] From this we might infer—rightly—that when he became a boarder at St Donatien's Seminary he was hardly a diligent scholar! He and his inseparable companion, his brother Paul, a year younger than himself, were high-spirited and adventurous: 'a real king of the playground' is how one of his teachers described little Jules.

Early in his childhood he showed his scientific interests. When offered a present he selected a model telegraph set—telegraphy having only recently been invented, these sets were greatly in vogue —but he was careful to insist that Paul must have one as well.

The Verne family had now moved off the Ile to a house on the mainland, with a country residence just out of town, at Chantenay. Though they had left their beloved island, however, life was still full of interest for the two young Vernes.

Progress had now reached Nantes, and the boys were delighted at the sight of some new means of transport. The 'White Ladies', as they were called, were spectacular omnibuses, drawn by four great

[1] Réné Ransson, *Jules Verne que j'ai connu.*

white horses, driven and escorted by white-clad coachmen and postilions, and rattling along over the *pavé* to the accompaniment of a musical-box actuated by the wheels.

Then appeared something even more exciting. Snorting and clanking and emitting clouds of smoke, while its paddles churned the waters of the Loire into foam, came a *pyroscaphe*, named from the Greek 'fire-ship', a clumsy tall-funnelled steamer. Such sights stimulated Jules Verne's imagination, and he delighted his schoolmates by sketching on the blackboard his idea of a steam-propelled omnibus—one account describes it as being hauled by a steam elephant!

At last, when about eleven, Jules got tired of merely dreaming about adventure and set out to find it. Meeting another small boy who was going to sea and heartily disliked the prospect, he offered to take his place and shipped as a cabin-boy on the *Coralie*, a three-master bound for the Indies.[1] (And what became of the real cabin-boy? As Verne put it of one of his characters: 'Where did he go? No matter. He won't appear in the story again.')

What exactly happened to Jules is not on record, nor what the captain said when he found that he had had foisted on him as one of his crew not a real cabin boy but a lad of good family and, what was more, the son of a lawyer who might be able to make trouble for him in the courts. Without being unduly brutal, he probably cured the stowaway of his romantic notions about sea-life by making sure he got the treatment, and performed the menial duties, that fall to a cabin-boy's lot.

So it must have been with mingled relief and apprehension that when they reached Paimboeuf, further down the Loire, Jules saw his father waiting for him on the quay: someone had seen him being rowed out to the *Coralie* and had passed on the word. On the one hand he was in for trouble: Pierre Verne was not the man to stand any nonsense. On the other hand here was an end to these cuffs and scoldings, this waiting on tough seamen who regarded their amateur cabin-boy not as an adventurous young hero but as a little fool who didn't know when he was well off.

Duly punished and scolded and cried over and forgiven, Jules assured his mother that henceforth he would travel only in his

[1] By one account, the East Indies; by another, the West!

imagination. This promise he kept not literally but in spirit, for travelling in his imagination became his life's work.

It says much for his character that even this disillusionment did not rob him of his love for the sea. It freed him from any ambition to serve before the mast. Nor did he, as did his brother Paul, aim at becoming a ship's officer: he may have realized that this would drag him away from his beloved books. Yet he still dreamed of voyages far away, to lonely tropical islands or the grey austerities of the Far North.

In spite of his day-dreaming, Jules could study seriously when he wished, and at the lycée that he and Paul attended he did quite well. At about the same time, too, the ink in his blood started to unclot. With the usual tendency of idealistic young authors to embark on highfalutin themes, he wrote a verse tragedy, but he met with the usual fate of idealistic young authors: his masterpiece was rejected and his friends and family ridiculed him. He relieved his feelings by writing a sonnet to the one girl who showed him a little sympathy —but she, alas, was not the girl whom he adored, but who did not return his love.

His education completed, he had to think about making a living. He had been invited to join a friend in Paris, but his father demurred and insisted on keeping him in his office to study law. Jules had to comply, but he did so with so bad a grace that his parents agreed to a compromise: under suitable chaperonage, he might go to Paris to study and take his preliminary examination there.

Having passed and returned home, he was still unreconciled to the career in his father's office for which he seemed destined, and he was moreover still suffering the twofold pangs of unappreciated genius and unrequited love. Normally high-spirited and full of fun, and rather good-looking, as Mme Allotte de la Fuÿe says, with his 'clean-cut profile, magnetic gaze, and flame-like lock of red-gold hair falling over his forehead', he slouched and sulked and was careless in his dress. When his brother Paul, after spending a few weeks on a coaster, set off for the Antilles, Jules became more intractable than ever. At last he really put his foot down and persuaded his parents, who indeed may have been glad to see the back of him, to let him return to Paris.

There, they imagined, he would go on studying law and pass his final exams; he was wise enough not to tell them that he was bent on a very different career. Paul had decided to be a deep-sea captain; Jules, with a number of manuscripts concealed in his trunk, was equally determined to win success as a playwright. Again, figuratively speaking, he had run away from home; but this time he was not going to be brought back in disgrace.

II
Aspiring Author

THE YEAR was 1848, and Paris was just recovering from one of its revolutions. Louis-Philippe had been dethroned, and the Second Republic was being officially inaugurated with impressive ceremony on the Place de la Concorde. Verne, who had solemnly promised his mother that he would be careful not to get mixed up in any riots, was naturally anxious to witness the spectacle. Having travelled by pyroscaphe to the rail-head at Tours,[1] he tried with a friend to gate-crash on to the special train which was taking the local National Guard to Paris. Foiled by the police, they arrived just in time, as his friend put it, to see 'the last candles guttering out in their sockets'.

In the true literary tradition, Verne and his friend lived frugally in cheap lodgings in the students' quarter on the Left Bank of the Seine. Apart from a light breakfast on rolls and milk, he could afford only one meal a day, and even so he could barely exist on the scanty allowance his father made him. Fortunately he and his friend found it not exasperating but amusing to have only the one dress-suit between them, so that they had to accept invitations out separately. Poverty did not keep Verne from the bookshops, however, and he bought a well-bound edition of Shakespeare even though it meant living for three days on dried prunes.

What did such privations matter? Here he was in Paris, in the very heart of the world of culture, and able sometimes to visit its famous salons. The political ones bored him, but there were others far more to his taste, where he might join in intellectual conversation, and even hope to meet the literary lions of France.

At last he was privileged to meet the greatest of all such lions, Victor Hugo; then a friendly professor of palmistry introduced him to another, Alexandre Dumas the elder. As Dumas prided himself as

[1] H. C. Harwood, in his introduction to an 'omnibus' edition of five Verne stories, points out that Verne, who foresaw so many triumphs of engineering, had never seen a railway-engine till he was twenty. But he had read about them, and he had travelled in the pyroscaphes.

much on his prowess as a cook as on his literary work. Verne had reason to be grateful for his hospitality; but he was still more grateful for the encouragement Dumas gave him, and for this opportunity of feeling himself in 'immediate contact' with literature. He was soon one of the 'bohemian' world of Paris, but his friends must have been amazed at the austerity of his personal life and at the sincerity of his religious beliefs.

The influence of Dumas and Hugo appears in one of his earliest stories, *The Fate of Jean Morénas*. In Monte Cristo vein, the scene opens in the convict-manned Toulon Dockyard, where a mysterious 'Man from Marseilles' is incredibly given the run of the place. So completely free from supervision is he that he contrives to slip a file into the hands of Morénas, sentenced to a long term of imprisonment for a crime he did not commit. A dramatic escape leads up to a climax which shows that Verne had already realized the value of a surprise ending, in which the hapless Jean displays a self-abnegation worthy of his namesake in *Les Misérables*.

Until it was included in the posthumous collection of Verne's shorter works, *Yesterday and Tomorrow*, this story failed to find publication, and no wonder, for it is obviously immature and unconvincing. Its author was more fortunate with his dramatic work, for Dumas, after reading three of his plays and rejecting two historical dramas, *The Gunpowder Plot* and *A Regency Tragedy*, 'edited' a slight one-act comedy, *Broken Straws*, and produced it at the Théâtre Historique. True, it paid its author nothing, but what did that matter? It was played twelve times!

Its plot is unimportant, a variation on that theme so dear to French dramatists, the 'eternal triangle'. It was hilariously welcomed by the bachelor club, the Onze Sans Femmes, which Verne had helped to found, and it won him a certain notoriety. This spread locally when the play was revived in Nantes, whose citizens regarded it with mixed feelings. While being—or pretending to be—shocked at its levity, they realized that it conferred a certain lustre on their town: whatever the circumstances, it is always exciting when, as they say, 'local boy makes good'.

The austere Pierre Verne shared both their pride and their misgivings, fearing that his talented son might become a 'dangerous' writer. Jules reassured him, explaining that this trifle was not meant to be taken seriously, and that he had far higher ideals in mind.

These ideas he discussed with Dumas; just as that author had based his work on history, so Verne would base his on the newly-discovered world of science. The encouragement Dumas gave him made up his mind: he distressed his father by refusing to be called to the bar and to enter the family business. 'I can make a good literary man but a bad lawyer,' he explained, 'for I can see things only on their humorous side.' With this end in view, he even hinted to his mother that a well-to-do wife would be an asset, but this hopeful idea came to nothing.

He was now reading more widely than ever. While he still enjoyed Scott and Fenimore Cooper, he had discovered another literary master who was to have far-reaching effects on his own work, Edgar Allan Poe. Here, in Baudelaire's translation, was just the sort of writer to appeal to him: a sensitive and evocative poet, and a discerning literary critic, Poe was also the father of the detective story, the pirate treasure story, the science fiction story—and the grandfather of the horror comic.

Some years later, in 1864, Verne contributed a thoughtful critique of Poe to the *Musée des Familles*. Entitled *Edgard Poë et ses Oeuvres*, it discusses several of that master's works. Most of Verne's comments can best be considered separately in relation to those of his stories which they influenced, but some deserve mention here.

Poe's *The Fall of the House of Usher*, 'the frightful experience of a young girl who is thought to be dead and is entombed, but who returns', gave Verne an interest in catalepsy: *The Facts in the Case of M. Valdemar*, in hypnotism; and, above all, *The Gold Bug*, in cryptography.

The ciphers Poe discussed, not only in that story but in his essay on the subject, were of the 'simple substitution' type, in which each letter of the alphabet is consistently represented throughout the message by another letter or by some arbitrary sign. These were far too elementary, and too easily solved, to satisfy Verne. His own ciphers, those which appear in several of his stories, are more complicated and difficult to decipher; one, as will be seen later, he wrongly thought to be completely undecipherable.

What most impressed him among Poe's works, however, was the strangely disquieting *Narrative of Arthur Gordon Pym of Nantucket*. In this story, which deserves reading both for its own sake and for its influence on Verne, the hero's fate is left uncertain; Poe,

says Verne, 'seemed to have deeply regretted this, and to have declined the task of filling in the gap'.

The conclusion of Verne's essay is worth quoting:

> 'Here then is a summary of the principal works of the American romancer; have I gone too far in describing them as strange and supernatural? Has he not created in real earnest a new form of literature, a form emanating from the *excessive* sensitiveness of his brain, to use one of his own words?
>
> 'In leaving on one side its incomprehensibility, what we have to admire in the works of Poe are the originality of his situations; the discussion of little-known facts; the observation of the more morbid faculties of man; the choice of his subjects; the personality, always strange, of his heroes; his own nervous and morbid temperament; his mode of expressing it by bizarre interjections. And yet, in the midst of these impossibilities, there sometimes appears a verisimilitude which grips the reader's credulity.
>
> 'May I now be permitted to direct attention to the materialistic aspect of his stories; never do we feel within them any sense of providential intervention. Poe never seems to recognize this; he claims to explain everything by physical law, which he is ready even to invent if need be; we never feel in him that faith which might bestow upon him the incessant contemplation of the supernatural.
>
> 'He creates his fantasy *coldly*, if I may express myself thus, and this wretched man is always an apostle of materialism. I imagine however that this is less due to his temperament than to the exclusively practical culture of the United States; he wrote, thought and dreamed in American, this positivist of a man; this tendency being acknowledged, we can admire his work.
>
> 'By his remarkable stories we can judge the state of over-excitement in which Edgar Poe lived; unfortunately his nature did not satisfy himself; and his excesses led him into the *terrible illness* of alcoholism which he had so well named and of which he died.'

One of Verne's early stories shows the influence both of Fenimore Cooper and of Poe. Its clumsy title, when it appeared in 1851 in the *Musée des Familles*, suggests that it was a 'historical study', but its English translator, W. H. G. Kingston, realized that it was nonfactual and simply called it *A Drama in Mexico: The First Vessels of the Mexican Navy.*

This rather blood-curdling yarn describes an alleged mutiny in the Spanish Navy followed by startling perils in the backwoods and culminating in a dramatic revenge. The two vessels captured by the mutineers, Verne said, became the kernel of the Mexican Navy, but whether there is any foundation for this statement I have been unable to ascertain.

Another of his stories, published in the same year and since re-titled *A Drama in the Air,* clearly shows the Poe influence: a pioneer aeronaut finds himself alone in the car of his balloon with a suicidal maniac.

The same influence is shown even more clearly in a long-short Verne story dated 1854.

Fascinated though he was by the possibilities of science, Jules Verne was too religious-minded to be misled by the 'brave new world' fantasies of some of its publicists. A devout Roman Catholic, he realized that in wrong hands it might become a presumptuous attempt to dethrone the Creator and enthrone 'mankind' in His stead.

What he called an 'insignificant occurrence' set his imagination at work. His watch had been lost, and while making their enquiries the police asked whether it had an escapement. 'Well,' laughed Verne, 'it certainly escaped me.'

This trivial pun suggested his extraordinary parable, *Master Zacharius,* described somewhat unconvincingly as a 'Genevan tradition'. Its central character, a Swiss clockmaker of the sixteenth century, is so proud of having invented the escapement, which regulates the timekeeper, that he compares it to the soul. This brings him under the power of a demon who appears as a human clock—it says much for Verne's descriptive powers and for the artistic skill of his illustrator, Théophile Gautier, that this grotesque conception seems not ludicrous but horrific.

Introducing himself as a colleague, the demon explains that it is his business to regulate the sun. 'I can hardly compliment you upon it,' Zacharius tells him reprovingly; 'your sun goes badly, and to make ourselves agree with it we sometimes have to put our clocks forward and sometimes back.'

After some horological shop-talk, the demon tempts the old man, who now looks like the 'fallen angel', into downright blasphemy: 'If God has created eternity, Master Zacharius has created time.'

The demon then demands the watchmaker's daughter in marriage, threatening reprisals, if he refuses, on all his handiwork. He is as bad as his word, for all the timepieces in Geneva, even the great clock in the Cathedral, stop or go wrong. But Zacharius is unmoved: prepared to sacrifice his own soul, he draws the line at sacrificing his daughter. The narrative ends dramatically among surroundings appropriate to the 'Gothic story', as the daughter and her betrothed wrestle spiritually with the demon for the old man's soul. . . .

This narrative reassured Pierre Verne, showing him that, in spite of his son's erratic ways and the unedifying theme of that play of his, the young genius was really sound at heart. He must have been further reassured by the pious ending of another Jules Verne long-short story, *Martin Paz* (1852); a somewhat melodramatic tale based on the clash of cultures in Peru and the attempts of the natives to free themselves from the Spanish yoke, it owed much to the water-colours of the Peruvian artist Mérino.

Both Jules' parents must have been comforted to learn that he had become secretary of the Théâtre Lyrique. His salary, though not over-generous, 1200 francs a year (about £45), was enough to keep the wolf from the door. The *Musée des Familles* was also encouraging, publishing all his stories, with the understandable exception of the ill-fated *Fate of Jean Morénas*. (One of these, which appeared in the *Musée* in 1852, was never published in book form: the sub-title of *Castles in California—Père qui roule n'amasse pas mousse*—is an untranslatable pun.)

Verne was now hard at work, writing mildly naughty farces for the Parisian stage with one hand, so to speak, and an edifying allegorical entertainment for a convent with the other. He was reading as widely and studying as hard as ever, and the incessant strain brought on bouts of insomnia, accompanied by bilious attacks, headaches, and earache; these culminated in a facial paralysis which contorted his mouth and closed his left eye.

Though he normally took little interest in politics, he may also have been perturbed, as a lover of freedom, by the coming to power of Napoleon III.

A visit he paid to Dunkirk may have improved his health while giving him a long-desired glimpse of the North Sea, and suggesting the first of his 'polar' stories, *A Winter Amid the Ice* (1855). A brig returns to the port flying a black flag, the symbol of a death on board: it is that of her captain, who was to have been married that very day; the log shows that he perished while trying to save another vessel from the Maëlstrom.

His father, the brig's owner, refuses to believe in his son's death and organizes a rescue expedition. Hardly has he left port than he finds a 'stowaway' on board; it is his own niece, the young captain's betrothed, who likewise feels convinced that he is still alive.

The girl is so far in advance of her time that, in preparation for wintering in the ice, she makes herself a pair of trousers (the artist was more squeamish, for he represented her in a skirt). Presumably, though this is not stated, she makes herself useful with the cooking and washing-up and the less exacting duties of a cabin-boy. On the whole, however, though a seaman assures her worried uncle that she would be their guardian angel, the 'little one' causes more trouble than she is worth. The scoundrelly mate is determined to win her for himself, so that to the inescapable perils of the ice-floes is added his treachery. . . .

With several stories published, and several plays in hand, Verne now felt he could regard himself as an established writer. Having saved a little cash, he relinquished his duties at the Théâtre Lyrique, with all the toil and worry they involved. Now, he flattered himself, he could devote all his time to literature. The incident which completely transformed his life surprised nobody more than himself.

Having attended an extremely formal wedding, he assured his family that 'never, never, could he seriously play a part in a ceremony of that sort'. Hardly a month later he went to Amiens to attend another wedding, that of one of his friends. The bride's sister was a charming young woman who captivated his heart at first sight.

A week or so later his family were taken aback to learn that Jules proposed to marry a widow with two small daughters, Mme Morel, *née* Honorine Anne Marie de Vianne. They were even more taken aback when he besought his father to buy him a share in a stockbroker's business.

Pierre Verne, who had been so disconcerted when his eldest son refused the law for literature, now found he was even more distressed that the same son should abandon the arts for a mere bourgeois business career. In vain did Jules expatiate on the financial prospects of stockbroking; the shrewd old lawyer was not convinced. But the pathetic words which concluded his son's letter touched the paternal heart: 'What I need is to be happy, neither more nor less.'

So, after the usual negotiations, financial and otherwise, without which no French marriage could be arranged, Pierre agreed to advance the sum needed to turn a budding genius into a respectable business man and to make his happiness possible. The wedding accordingly took place, with the minimum of pomp and circumstance, in Paris, on 10 January 1857.

While the bridegroom was installing his wife and his two newly-acquired daughters in what had been his bachelor flat on the fifth floor of a Parisian house, Pierre Verne took his own family back to Nantes. He was distressed not only by what were, by his standards, a slapdash ceremony and wedding breakfast, but by what seemed his son's abandonment of his ideals. He was unmoved by Jules' assurance that he could combine stockbroking with literature, for he knew enough of affairs to doubt the possibility of this. He may have felt, too, that his new daughter-in-law, who seemed to have her head screwed on the right way, would see that, now that he had a wife and family to support, her husband kept his nose to the grindstone.

III
Frustrated Ambitions

If Pierre Verne really thought that Jules would give up his literary work now that he had gone into business, or that his wife Honorine would induce him to do so, he had under-estimated his son's capabilities and her new daughter-in-law's outlook.

With the energy he could always show when he wished, Jules Verne set out to follow his two careers at once. Rising at five, he would gulp down a cup of coffee and a mouthful of food and write until it was time to go to the Exchange at ten. While engaged on his literary projects he was willing, as he explained, to 'toil like a beast of burden', whereas on 'Change he was, as one of his colleagues commented, 'better at banter than at business'. He gravitated to a clique of literary-minded stockbrokers whom he delighted with his wit but amazed with the seriousness he always showed in discussing religious questions.

How he contrived to make a living is not clear. Perhaps his colleagues found his society so congenial that they would give him useful tips or pass on an occasional client. Perhaps he was drawing on his wife's dowry or being subsidized by her family. Certainly he was on better terms with them than many husbands are with their in-laws; indeed, Amiens became more of a home to him than his birthplate, Nantes.

What was he working at? None of his published stories seem to date from this period, though he was diligently accumulating material and filing it in the large desk which accompanied him during the frequent moves which his restless mind drove him to make. It held two special sections, one for humour and another for notes on science, whose developments he followed carefully.

He was still a dramatist. In 1859 he collaborated in an operetta, *The Inn in the Ardennes*, and in 1860 Offenbach directed a Verne musical comedy, *Monsieur de Chimpanzé*. In this Mme de la Fuÿe explains, 'a monkey dressed up as a man finds his way into high society, where he behaves a good deal better than most of those around him'. In 1861 Verne collaborated in a three-act comedy for the Vaudeville Theatre, *Eleven Days' Siege*: its rather slight point turns upon a technicality in the French marriage-laws.

In the summer of 1859 he broke his promise to travel only in his imagination. A friend, who was an agent for a shipping-line, invited him to a free return voyage to Scotland, with the opportunity of greeting his parents as he passed through Nantes.

Admirer of Sir Walter Scott and lover of the romance of the Highlands as he was, he jumped at the chance. The semi-fictional account he wrote of the trip has never been published, but it is interestingly quoted from in Kenneth Allott's biography, and years later it supplied background and local colour for Verne's two Scottish stories.

Jules was in an appreciative mood which made even commonplace details romantic, so that in the light shining from the binnacle during the night, 'the vessel seemed to be steered by a supernatural hand turning a luminous wheel'. When, crossing England overland on his way north, he came in sight of the Lake District, he hailed it, a little prematurely, as 'the country of Fergus and McGregor'.

In Edinburgh he and his friend went sightseeing and listened to the traditional Scottish ballads and the bagpipes; thence they travelled through the Loch Lomond region and the Trossachs. Delighted with the scenery and its legends, Verne was no less impressed with the coal-mining areas and especially with the desolation around a worked-out pit, which he described so effectively in *Black Diamonds*. He was, as Allott points out, one of the first to realize the sadness of wrecked and abandoned machinery.

The depression this wreckage produced was dissipated when he and his friend reached the Western Isles. The Hebrides delighted him, especially Fingal's Cave in the Island of Staffa. He extolled its beauties in *The Green Ray* and commemorated the whole tour by a poem in *Black Diamonds* which defies any attempt at metrical translation. Its refrain runs:

Beaux lacs aux ondes dormantes
Gardez à jamais
Vos légendes charmantes,
Beaux lacs écossais.[1]

[1] The whole poem is quoted in the appendix to the Fitzroy Edition of *Black Diamonds*.

Even while revelling in the wonders and beauties of nature of deploring the aftermath of a worked-out coal-mine, Verne could still regard them with the impersonal eye of a student of science. His delight in the charms of Staffa was increased by his interest in its remarkable geological structure, and he eagerly sought information about the lay of the coal-measures and the technique of mining.

As they passed through London on their way home, Verne was impressed at the sight of Brunel's immense steamship, the *Great Eastern*, then under construction. He made up his mind that when he achieved success he would cross the Atlantic as one of her passengers.

At times, as he admitted to his father, he doubted that success; hard as he had toiled, he had scarcely achieved anything. At times, as he assured his wife, he felt certain of it. Fortunately he had chosen an ideal partner: had she systematically discouraged his ambitions and kept urging him to devote himself to earning a living, he would have found things very difficult. But she seems either to have been resigned to, or delighted with, her marriage to an intellectual of real promise, even though he put his work before everything except his Faith. No doubt he was temperamental, but she was prepared to put up with his vagaries.

Although she was now expecting her third, and his first, child, she raised no objection when he accepted his friend's invitation to another sea-trip, a six-weeks cruise on a cargo-boat to Norway. They visited several of the fjords, and Jules was especially delighted when, wildly improbable though this is, he thought he had caught a doubtful glimpse of Iceland!

Cutting short his trip by omitting a visit to Copenhagen, he reached Paris just in time for the birth of his only child, his son Michel. Overjoyed as he was to become a father, he soon learned, as many others have learned, that it is not conducive to exacting brain work to have a young baby under the same roof.

Seeking refuge in a literary club, *Le Cercle de la Presse Scientifique*, he spent much time with a special friend, a man so extraordinary that Verne later used him as a character in his moon-travel stories. This was Félix Tournachon, who after several vicissitudes had become a successful photographer, for professional reasons taking the pseudonym of Nadar.

The two had much in common, for Verne's description of Michel

Ardan, in *From the Earth to the Moon*, might equally be applied to himself: 'He was one of those originals which nature sometimes invents in the freak of a moment, and of which she then breaks the mould.' They shared a special interest in aeronautics and aviation, and exchanged ideas to their mutual advantage.

Verne's interest was purely theoretical: he had already written an article on the subject in the *Musée des Familles*. Nadar's was severely practical: his ultimate aim was to construct a 'flying machine', as aircraft heavier-than-air used to be called, and he hoped to raise the necessary funds by making remunerative ascents in a huge balloon he was planning, appropriately called the *Géant*—also discussed by Verne in the *Musée*.

Stimulated by his conversations with Nadar, Verne devoted himself to the compilation of a manuscript dealing with the possible uses of balloons in exploration. Its exact nature is uncertain: it may well have been non-fictional or semi-fictional, the sort of thing that might now be called a 'documentary'.

He took immense trouble over this work, the most ambitious and important he had ever written. He was correspondingly disappointed when every publisher to whom he sent it returned it with the equivalent of a rejection-slip.

His annoyance may have been vented in a satire he wrote about this time (1863) on what he regarded as the besetting sin of American life, aptly summed up in its title, *The Humbug*. Its hero, who might almost be called an anti-hero, is a super-Barnum who has achieved notoriety by announcing that he has unearthed the skeleton of a forty-foot prehistoric humanoid giant, and who then, when the time comes to display it publicly, calmly explains that it has been destroyed by some animal! This accident, he declares, has ruined him; a subscription-list is opened for his benefit, and he keeps his reputation as 'The Most Enterprising Man in the New World'. Verne sums up the moral bitterly:

> 'I came to the conclusion that the future of artistes without any talent, singers without any voice, dancers without any legs, and high-jumpers without any rope, would have been simply frightful if Columbus had not discovered America.'

This story is unlikely ever to be translated and indeed never achieved publication even in France until it was, most injudiciously, included in the posthumous collection, *Yesterday and Tomorrow*. Verne indeed may never have meant to publish it: he may simply have been 'letting off steam' by expressing his opinion of 'writers without talent' who somehow contrive to get into print.

That indeed was what his own treatise on ballooning was failing to do. 'What a lot of papers!' Honorine had written to her mother-in-law as he was finishing it. 'Let's hope they don't end up in the fire!'

These words seemed also prophetic, for Verne was losing patience. After another rejection he gave up hope. Here was his precious manuscript, on which he had lavished so much care, in which he had placed so much faith, refused once again! With a dramatic gesture—and maybe with a yell of despair—he flung it into the fire.

IV
Victorious with the *Victoria*

HAD Verne been alone when he committed his manuscript to the flames, the whole course of the world's literature, and indeed of the world's history, would have been very different.

Fortunately, however, his wife was in the room, and at the risk of her fingers she pulled the precious document off the fire: there was still one publisher, she reminded him, that he hadn't tried. So when the scorched sheaf of papers had been given a new cover, he set off again, perhaps gloomily prognosticating another failure, although with renewed hope rising in his heart.

No. 18 Rue Jacob was a bookshop and publishing house. It was also the home of Verne's namesake, Jules Hetzel, not only a publisher of standing but an author, under the name of P. J. Stahl, of several children's stories, 'full of humour and witty *bonhomie*'. He was always on the search for new talent, not so much from a commercial point of view as because his great aim was the advancement of literature.[1]

A late worker, and a late riser, Hetzel was not yet up when his visitor arrived, so he had to deal with him from his bed. With a word of explanation, Verne handed over his manuscript; asked to return in a fortnight's time, he bowed and took his leave.

A fortnight later he returned and again Hetzel interviewed him from his bed. Once more Verne heard the well-known words he had half expected and half feared: 'I regret that, in spite of your work's undoubted merit, I am unable . . .'.

Snatching up his ill-used manuscript, he was about to flounce out of the room in a huff, when Hetzel called him back. Yes, the work as it stood was unpublishable, but only in its present form: there were great possibilities in it. He went into some detail, discussing its weak passages and pointing out where it could be expanded or curtailed. For there was a splendid story in this idea of exploring

[1] A. Parménie and C. Bonnier de la Chapelle, *Histoire d'un Éditeur et de ses Auteurs*.

unknown Africa by balloon; what was more, Verne showed clearly that he had it in him to be a great story-teller. Could he develop the idea in fictional form?

Yes, he could and he would. Dashing home full of delight, he sat down at his desk and grasped his pen, no longer 'toiling like a beast of burden' but rejoicing in a congenial task like a free man. (And his duties at the Exchange? They had presumably passed out of his mind.)

His theme was certainly original. Soaring from Zanzibar and taking advantage of the trade-winds, an idea Verne had derived from a paper read to the French Academy of Sciences by a military engineer, Captain Meusnier, a balloon would make an exploratory flight across Africa. 'As to where this will end,' the press is represented as saying, 'Providence only knows.'

Not that the explorers were to be at the mercy of the trade-winds. No successful method yet having been invented of steering a balloon, or even of making it rise and fall at will without losing its vital supply of gas, Verne had to devise one that would be practicable—on paper, at any rate. His method is very distantly related to that used, with fatal results, by the first victims of ballooning. It is summed up by the maniac in *A Drama in the Air*:

> 'Pilatre des Roziers set out with Romain from Boulogne on 13th June, 1785. To his gas balloon he affixed a montgolfier hot-air apparatus, so as to dispense, no doubt, with the need to lose gas or throw out ballast. It was like putting a furnace under a powder-barrel.'

The weakness of the method, Verne realized, lay in the use of an open balloon over a naked flame. But suppose the balloon were sealed, so that instead of an explosive mixture of hydrogen and air it contained pure hydrogen? Then it would presumably be quite safe.

So he imagined an ingenious apparatus whose description, to quote Kenneth Allott, 'comforts and reassures the reader even as he skips the passage'.

The balloon is hermetically sealed, but a metal tube from its base leads down into the car, where it passes through a furnace. Here, expanding into a cone, it can be heated by an oxy-hydrogen flame fed by the gases produced when water is decomposed by a powerful electric battery. Thence it leads upwards nearly into the balloon's top.

Normally the balloon is half-inflated with hydrogen, which also fills the tube; being then in equilibrium with the air, it rests gently on the ground. When the jet, safely enclosed in the furnace, is lighted, it heats the tube and cone, making the hydrogen within them expand. Rising into the upper part of the balloon, the expanded hydrogen produces in the tube a partial vacuum which draws in more gas from the balloon's lower part.

A continuous circulation is thus set up, and the expansion of the gas inflates the balloon and makes it rise. The hotter the furnace, the higher soars the balloon. When the jet is extinguished the gas cools and contracts and the balloon descends. To keep it at the same height, all that is needed is to regulate the heat.

Whether this ingenious method would work is uncertain; if a little air were to seep into the balloon, results might be unfortunate as traces of the explosive mixture passed into the intensely-heated cone. Certainly it never seems to have been tried, though the use of helium instead of hydrogen would obviate any risk of explosion.

Verne now had to incorporate the method into a story. He knew of the daring explorations of Africa made (on foot) by the British and of the splendid work of the Royal Geographical Society. So the narrative opens with an account of the enthusiastic reception which the Society gives to an experienced English explorer, Dr Samuel Fergusson, and of his laconic response:

> 'He walked towards the chair placed ready for him; then standing with an air of determination, he raised the forefinger of his right hand towards the sky, opened his mouth, and pronounced this one word:
>
> '"Excelsior!"'

So completely won over is the most sceptical of his opponents that he moves the insertion of the Doctor's speech 'in its entirety' in the Society's *Proceedings.* The scene ends with a banquet held in the Doctor's honour, when the guests drink to the memory, in alphabetical order, 'of the celebrated travellers who had made themselves illustrious on African soil'—over a hundred in all.

Having relieved his mind with this touch of satire, omitted in some of the English translations, Verne proceeds in more serious vein. There is a touch of Walter Scott influence here, for the Doctor's companion, the intrepid Scottish hunter Dick Kennedy, resembles

Halbert Glendinning in *The Monastery*. The two are accompanied by the Doctor's manservant, Joseph Wilson, loyal, intelligent, and courageous. 'If Fergusson must be the head and Kennedy the arm, Joe would be the hand of the expedition.'

The interplay of the three characters enables Verne to liven up the narrative with their talk and, without holding up the story unduly, to insert the geographical details in which he delighted, as the Doctor explains them to his less erudite companions.

Granted the practicability of the invention on which it depends, the balloon's voyage keeps within the bounds of possibility. When his heroes cross regions of which something is known, their experiences are based on recorded fact; when they reach unexplored areas, conditions are such as travellers might expect to find; the perils they encounter arise not from fantastic monsters but from Africa's birds and beasts, its natural conditions and savage tribes. Verne was no Rider Haggard, to fill unknown Africa with strange white races and imperious immortal queens; nor was he an Edgar Rice Burroughs: when a cry for help reaches the explorers' ears it comes not from the long-lost daughter of some white missionary captured by the natives, but from the missionary himself.

Yet the story is full of excitement. While making his narrative plausible, Verne gives his heroes plenty of adventure, writing so vividly that his readers can feel that they are sharing their experiences and facing their privations and hazards. He adds verisimilitude by giving the exact bearings of several points on the route, so that this can be charted on the map. Saluted by the guns of its escort vessel, H.M.S. *Resolute*, the *Victoria*, as Dr Fergusson patriotically calls his balloon, rises on 18 April 1862 from Koumbeni, an islet off Zanzibar. Where and how it finally descends the reader may learn from a typical Vernian surprise ending.

Incredible as it may seem, the story was completed within a fortnight! Hetzel was delighted with it; here was what every publisher longs for but seldom finds, a masterpiece. Nor was it a mere commercial 'best seller': admirably written, lucid in style, with vivid descriptions, lively conversation, and pleasant touches of humour, it above all conveyed a lofty moral idealism.

Subject to some further alterations, including the omission of irrelevant detail about 'Joe', he accepted it out of hand. Then he asked its author if he had any more books in mind.

Verne, who had not yet shaken off the illusions of his youth, explained enthusiastically that he wanted to shake modern society right down to its foundations by the boldness and cruelty of his descriptions.[1] Hetzel had to bring him down to earth like a deflated balloon before he could enlarge on his own plans.

He was about, he explained, to launch a new magazine, whose purpose was aptly conveyed by its title, *Le Magazin d'Education et de Récréation.* Could Verne undertake to write two stories a year, or their equivalent, to be serialized in this and then to appear in book form?

Again Verne could, and he would. As they discussed the possibilities of this venture, each stimulated the other's imagination until it soared like the balloon *Victoria* itself. Finally, Verne was placed under a life-long contract to provide those two books in return for an annual payment of 20,000 francs (roughly equivalent to £750). Here, by the standards of the time, was affluence indeed!

Having delighted Honorine with these good tidings, Verne went off to the Exchange to bid a dramatic farewell to his former colleagues. One of them, claiming to have a reliable memory, later contributed to the *Temps* an article which, he said, reproduced its exact words. Like Dr Fergusson's famous speech, already quoted, to the Royal Geographical Society, it deserves to be reproduced 'in its entirety':

> 'Boys, I'm leaving you. I've had an idea, the sort of idea, they say, which ought to come to everybody once a day, though it's come to me only once in my lifetime, the sort of idea which should make anybody's fortune. If it succeeds I shall have come across a gold-mine, and then I shall go on ceaselessly writing, while you fellows go on buying shares the day before they fall and selling them the day before they rise. I'm leaving the Exchange. Good evening, boys.'

Now he had burned his boats; he was committed to living by his pen for the rest of his life.

Meanwhile the real-life equivalent of his balloon—though it lacked the special device he had imagined—was still under construction. Completed in October 1863, it made three spectacular but short-lived flights, and on the third it was destroyed in a crash-landing in Ger-

[1] H. Barlet, *L'Auteur des Voyages Extraordinaires.*

many. Fortunately neither of its occupants, Nadar or his wife, was seriously injured.

Nadar's *Géant* had been destroyed. But in the world's imagination Verne's *Victoria* was triumphantly soaring aloft. Published in the New Year of 1863, the story of its flight became the first of his famous *Strange Journeys* (*Les Voyages Extraordinaires*), later dramatically sub-titled *Worlds Known and Unknown* (*Les Mondes Connus et Inconnus*).

Meantime it was being translated into many tongues and appearing in many lands. It is still being read and enjoyed; surely there are few literates who have not at least heard of *Five Weeks in a Balloon*. Those five weeks have now lasted a good hundred years.

V

Founding a New Art-form

AMONG Verne's many interests was Arctic exploration, and he was especially stirred by the mystery which had long surrounded the fate of Sir John Franklin and by Lady Franklin's efforts to rescue him. In seeking the North-west Passage, as in exploring Africa, the British had moreover been foremost, but now they had to face a possible rivalry, for Elisha Kane of the U.S. Navy had discovered a channel west of Greenland which seemed likely to lead to the North Pole. This, and not the Passage, might henceforth become the explorers' goal.

Here was splendid material for an adventure story. Conditions beyond Greenland were almost unknown, and there might be an 'open sea' completely free from ice in the Far North: had not Henry Hudson, in the seventeenth century, attempted to reach China by way of the Pole? All that was needed was a plot, a central character to hold the narrative together—and, of course, a ship.

So the next of the *Strange Journeys, The English at the North Pole*[1] (1866), begins by describing a vessel of unusual build. Much speculation arises as to her destination: not even her mate, Shandon, nor her scientist, Dr Clawbonny, know it. Nor do they know who her captain is to be, for his detailed instructions for her construction have arrived anonymously. So the brig *Forward* sets sail on 5 April 1860, 'destination unknown'.

It remains unknown up to the actual moment of sailing, when the captain's dog appears on deck with a letter between his teeth; this too is anonymous, merely giving general instructions to sail northwards west of Greenland. Later orders, appearing seemingly from nowhere, direct the vessel to make for Smith's Sound, Kane's suggested approach to the Pole.

These mysterious instructions tell on Shandon's nerves, and he loses his grip on the crew, who are on the verge of mutiny just as the vessel is about to be smashed in the moving ice.

[1] Simply called in the Fitzroy Edition *At the North Pole*.

Then, in the nick of time, the captain appears. Hitherto passing as one of the crew, he takes command and saves the ship. Unfurling the British Flag, he announces dramatically that it shall fly above the North Pole. 'My name is enough,' he declares. 'It stands for energy and patriotism. I am Captain Hatteras!'

That name was already notorious, the Captain being fanatically regardless of human suffering in his determination to reach the Pole before his detested rivals, the Americans. Hence all this mystery: had his identity been known, hardly a man would have been found willing to serve under him.

For a time he overcomes the crew's misgivings, and Clawbonny with one or two others are devoted to him. But mutiny, abetted by Shandon, is still smouldering: when fuel runs out and Hatteras and his followers have gone to look for some opencast coal, the rebels not merely abandon ship but set her on fire.

So, far from being at the North Pole, as the book's title promises, the English seem unable ever to reach it. With hardly any fuel or food, and hampered by a half-dead stranger whom they have found buried in the snow, they are six degrees from the Pole. But Hatteras is undismayed:

> '"Friends! The cowards have fled! The strong will succeed! Johnson and Bell, you have courage! Doctor, you have science! And I—I have faith. The North Pole is there. Let us get on with our work!"'

With greater experience Verne would have made this story part one of a two-volumed book and continued it as Part II. Instead he seems to have felt that his contract to supply two stories a year demanded two different titles. The story's second part appeared as *The Wilderness of Ice*, both being combined in book form as *The Adventures of Captain Hatteras* (1866). He afterwards abandoned this clumsy method, and his longer books mostly appeared in two or three volumes under the same title (though in some English translations each part bears a different name).

The second book deals with the further efforts of Hatteras to reach the Pole, and with his rivalry with the American explorer whom he had rescued. He meets with appalling difficulties and perils. Though Verne's description of conditions in the Far North is now known to be wildly incorrect, he could not have foreseen this, and he was justified in regarding them as possible.

Hetzel had pressed Verne to introduce a French character into the story, but he had refused, insisting that the whole expedition must be English; he compromised, however, by devoting a chapter to the tragic death of the heroic French explorer Lieutenant Bellot.

Verne also refused another of Hetzel's suggestions. How could he bring Hatteras back to England? 'What would he do there? Obviously he ought to die at the Pole: the volcano is the only tomb worthy of him!'[1] Though later he modified this decision, his narrative works up to a highly dramatic ending.

Even before Verne had completed this story he was planning its successor. The fallacious theory on which he based it is expounded by Dr Clawbonny:

> '"In recent times it has even been suggested that there are great chasms at the Poles; it is through these that there emerges the light which forms the Aurora, and you can get down through them into the interior of the earth."'

Though not the first to make fictional use of the hollow-earth theory, Verne was the first to place his narrative on a scientific basis. He gained much technical information from the French seismologist Charles Sainte-Claire Deville, and he had heard it suggested that the Italian volcanoes might be connected by underground fissures. Why should not these lead to an immense subterranean cavity, which he could people with the extinct animals of the distant past?

Here was the basis for his next book, *Journey to the Centre of the Earth* (1864). It is related in the first person by Axel, a German student whose upbringing recalls that of his compatriot Werner, a savant whose sheer brilliance as a mineralogist seriously retarded the progress of geological science.

Axel's uncle, Otto Lidenbrock, is an amusing caricature of what the French then regarded as the typical German professor, cranky but erudite, irascible but essentially good-hearted, and on no account to be taken seriously. Lidenbrock is also a polyglot and a bibliophile, immensely excited at his purchase of an ancient Icelandic chronicle. His excitement knows no bounds when there drops out of it a dirty scrap of parchment, bearing a number of Runic characters.

[1] Parménie and de la Chapelle.

Here the Poe influence is obvious, for these characters form a cipher. Having transliterated them into modern letters and placed them in correct order, the Professor finds them still so incomprehensible that he is about to give up in despair.

Then Axel, whose love for Lidenbrock's ward, Graüben, has accidentally leaked out during the process, chances to hit on the solution. Translated from its original dog-Latin, the message runs:

> 'Descend into that crater of Sneffels Yocul which the shadow of Scartaris touches just before the calends of July, audacious traveller, and you will reach the centre of the earth. I have done it. Arne Saknussemm.'

The professor explains that that Saknussemm[1] was a sixteenth-century alchemist, and announces his intention of accepting the challenge.

Axel quails at the prospect, but when Graüben promises him her hand on his return he nerves himself for the ordeal: his is the true courage that masters fear, and when once underground he gets so enthusiastic for the technical aspects of the adventure that he hardly gives her a thought. So the exploration of the underworld proceeds, with a wealth of adventure paving the way for one of the best of Verne's surprise endings on the very last page.

'This *Journey to the Centre of the Earth* caused a tremendous sensation. It was put into print and translated into every language throughout the world.' These words, put into the mouth of Axel, are literally true. As the story can still be enjoyed, even now that we are hardened to 'strange journeys' and know its central idea to be fallacious, we can well imagine what enthusiasm it aroused when its theoretical basis was credible and science fiction was otherwise unknown! It is brilliantly written, its abundant technical material being skilfully woven into the story; when contemporary disputes about the existence of 'antediluvian man' were finally settled, Verne took advantage of the decision to add an additional chapter, in which that existence is made abundantly clear.[2]

[1] The Icelandic Embassy regard this name as fictitious, but suggest that it may be derived from that of a famous Icelandic scholar of the seventeenth/eighteenth century, Arni Magnusson.

[2] Etienne Cluzel, 'Jules Verne et la Préhistoire'. Included in the *Bulletin du Bibliophile et de Bibliothécaire*, 1957.

The book made many of its readers aware for the first time of the long history of our planet and its inhabitants. It led, and is still leading, some to become geologists, some to become speleologists or cavers, some to become science fiction addicts, and some to become all three. It also kept its author's name in the limelight and made his admirers wonder if his next book could possibly be as original and exciting as this.

That next book came from an idea used by Edgar Allan Poe. He had written a burlesque space-travel story, *The Unparalleled Adventure of One, Hans Pfaal*, representing its hero as reaching the moon's surface in a balloon; if the reader had not already guessed this already, its last paragraph reveals that it is a hoax.

Preposterous as the story was, the idea behind it was just the sort of thing to appeal to Verne. Might it not really be practicable to send to the moon, if not what is now called a space-ship, at all events, again to use the modern term, some sort of space-capsule? If a gun could be made large enough, might it not launch a projectile with a reasonable hope of crossing the gap between earth and moon? This, after all, was less than 250,000 miles! Here were the makings of another story, and now Verne had to imagine the sort of artillerymen who might construct the gun.

Greatly as he detested the 'Barnum' aspect of American life, he realized that this was only a misleading by-product of the transatlantic enterprise and energy he so greatly admired; and he had heard amusing stories of the tendency to clot into societies of like-minded individuals which many Americans show.

Here were just the enthusiasts he had in mind. With a suggestion of the macabre which might well have come from Poe, he imagines the Gun Club of Baltimore, all of whose members have first-hand knowledge of ballistics, and most of whom had been shockingly mutilated as a result of the American Civil War.

These veterans are shown as deploring not the horrors of war but the futilities of peace: gone were those delightful days when, to quote the armless Bilsby: 'One invented a gun and hardly was it cast when he hastened to try it in the face of the enemy.' Giving up as hopeless a scheme for provoking a war with Britain, they are on the point of dissolving the Club, as its purpose no longer exists.

Then their President, Impey Barbicane, rekindles their enthusiasm with a proposal to fire a shot to the moon. Unprecedented as this proposal is, it arouses world-wide enthusiasm and support, only the British remaining aloof.

The satire of the opening chapters vanishes as Verne warms up to his task, and he treats the scheme with increasing seriousness. The astronomers of a leading observatory having decided that it is practicable and given the necessary technical details, the Club appoints a committee to draw up its plans; its secretary, who now would be called the venture's 'back-room boy', is an amusing figure, the one-armed J. T. Maston.

The size and weight of the projectile, the dimensions and siting of the Columbiad—the giant gun which is to fire it—the nature and quantity of the explosive, all are settled, though there seems to be little attempt to correlate the weight of the projectile with the amount of the propellant. At last 'The plan was drawn up and all that remained was to put it into execution.

'"A mere matter of detail, a trifle," said J. T. Maston.'

Then the construction of the space gun is described with almost a documentary precision.

Now come two unforeseen developments. A leading armourer, Captain Nicholl, denounces the scheme as foolhardy and opposes it vehemently. Then a telegram arrives from France:

> 'Substitute for your spherical shell a cylindrical-conical projectile. I shall go inside. . . . Michel Ardan.'

The surname of this would-be astronaut—his Christian name is that of Verne's own son—reveals his real-life prototype. 'Ardan' is anagrammatic for 'Nadar', the professional name of Verne's friend, Félix Tournachon, who declared himself amazed at the honour thus conferred upon him. Certainly it was not undeserved, for Nadar was the sort of person who might well volunteer to fly to the moon had such an exploit then been possible.

Ardan is no mere passenger. In a spirited public debate, which enables Verne to expound much technical matter readably, he confutes the hostile Captain Nicholl, and when Nicholl and Barbicane are to meet in a duel he averts bloodshed by a brilliant stratagem: he simply invites them to join him in the projectile and see whether it reaches the moon or not! (And nobody seems to notice that this larger pay-load would demand a corresponding increase in the propellant!) With, it turns out later, rather surprising results, he assumes responsibility for what might be called the domestic side of the expedition, its food and other amenities.

The idea of a space-gun is now known to be utterly impracticable: projectile and occupants would be not merely crushed but volatilized by the sheer pressure of air. Verne could not possibly have known this, however, and he shows a surprising prescience in some of his details. It may be only coincidental that the emplacement of his Columbiad, at Tampa Town, Florida, is almost on the same latitude as Cape Canaveral, and that the dimensions of the telescope he places on the Rocky Mountains differ only by four inches from those of the giant instrument at Palomar. But it was more than guess-work when he foresaw the experimental use of animals before human space-flight was attempted, and when he realized that the only method of changing the course of a space-ship is by means of rockets.

When it appeared in 1865 *From the Earth to the Moon* was such a success that it demanded a sequel describing the actual space-flight. Several years elapsed, however, before this appeared. Mean-time the story had evoked some curious responses. The most fan-tastic consisted of offers from literal-minded people to accompany Verne in an expedition to the moon, and some of these suggestions came from ladies whose aims were hardly platonic. Verne dismissed such advances cynically: 'What, play Adam to some daughter of Eve up there? No, thank you! I'd be meeting a selenite serpent next!'

More serious were the technical criticisms of the calculations on which the moon-flight had been based. Verne, when he had them checked by a distant cousin, the mathematician Professor Henri Garcett, was not unduly disconcerted by the disclosure of a serious error: no allowance had been made for the resistance of the air! What was more, the second book was totally inconsistent with the surprise ending of the first.

He found no difficulty in slurring over such details in his second space-travel story, *Round the Moon* (1870). He merely explained that the astronomers had been mistaken when they thought they saw the projectile doomed for ever to circle aimlessly round the moon: they must have seen something else! As for the mathematical error, he said airily that this had been compensated by an under-estimate of the propelling power of the explosive.

It must be admitted that, judged by the modern standards of astrogation, Verne's ideas of space-flight were a little lacking in precision. . . .

Such faults are forgotten in the brilliance of the narrative. The experiences of the three space-men are described vividly, from the appalling shock of blast-off to their calm resignation when they realize that their efforts to reach the moon have failed and that they are confronting an inevitable death.

During their flight they bask in the warmth of the sunshine and shiver when it is intercepted by the moon. They study at close range the details of the moon's surface. The reader shares their awe at the wonder and beauty of the sky as seen from beyond the atmosphere:

> 'The heavens, thus seen, presented a new aspect, and one of which the human eye could never have dreamed. . . . Long did the three friends watch without speaking, though united in heart, while the projectile sped onwards with ever-decreasing speed.'

With Michel Ardan in the projectile the space-flight could not lack cheerfulness. There is the hilarious moment when, arrived at the 'neutral point' where the gravitational pulls of earth and moon cancel out, the astronauts pass into the weightless condition now known as 'free fall'. When Nicholl lets slip a glass it hangs motionless in mid-air; so do the other objects, even the dog, when they are left unsupported:

> 'Suddenly Michel, making a leap, left the floor and stayed suspended in the air. . . . His two friends joined him at once and the three formed a miraculous "Ascension" in the centre of the projectile.
>
> '"We're passing the neutral line!" cried Michel. "Then let's do as the sailors do when they cross the equator. . . . Let's wet it!"'

There are obvious inconsistencies here. Michel Ardan's leap would not leave him 'suspended in the air'; unless an astronaut is securely strapped down he will need a crash-helmet. Nor would he be able to pour out the wine, for it too would be weightless; so he and his friends would have to 'wet' the line unromantically by sucking their drink up through a straw.

Moreover, the state of 'free fall' would occur not merely at the neutral point where the two gravitations cancel out; it would prevail throughout the whole voyage. Nor would the projectile reverse itself as the pull of the moon, overcoming that of the earth, attracted the heavy base. As no means of stabilizing it had been provided it would sway about and overturn unpredictably, to the occupants' extreme discomfort. Verne can hardly be blamed for such errors: when he wrote astrogatory science had not yet begun.

The projectile's failure to reach its destination is described as due to its being deflected off-course by the gravitational pull of a large earth-circling meteor, a smaller 'second moon' which just fails to collide with it. Not only has it been calculated, however, that even if such a meteor existed its pull would not be great enough for such an effect; there is in fact no such 'second moon'. Professor Clyde W. Tombaugh, who discovered the planet Pluto, made a special search for such small earth-satellites but failed to find any. This was another result that Verne could not possibly have foreseen.

His only crass mistake—really he should have known better—is the statement he attributes to Barbicane, that whenever the sun sets on the moon the earth rises over the opposite horizon. The sun would indeed rise and set; but as the moon always keeps practically the same face turned earthwards, as is explained at some length in the earlier book, the earth, as seen from the moon, would neither rise nor set but would stay poised in the sky, with only a slight to-and-fro movement due to the moon's libration.

Again, these blemishes do not spoil a stirring and thought-provoking narrative, and are mentioned only to show how the author's work looks in the light of subsequent research. It says much for his technical competence that his errors are so few; he did not completely foresee the effects of free fall, but how many of his contemporaries would have realized that such a condition could possibly exist?

Verne had now founded not only science fiction but one of its specialized branches. Other stories of journeys to the moon had been either fanciful or satiric, but he felt that space travel was to be dealt with seriously. He had thus shown that, like science fiction generally, it was compatible with brilliant characterization, vivid description, humour, awe at the beauties of nature, and sincere religious faith.

VI
Hard Work and a Holiday

UP TO 1865 Verne's works had shown a sort of imaginative crescendo, taking their readers across Africa, to the Pole, into the interior of the earth, and towards the moon; each formed an advance on its predecessor. If his public expected his next 'strange journey' to lead them still further afield, they were disappointed.

The Children of Captain Grant, 1868 (recently filmed as *In Search of the Castaways*), deals with better-known regions. It was the longest story he had so far written, running to three volumes, and it is the nearest approach to a mystery story he ever wrote, the problem however being not to discover 'whodunit' but 'ware wozzit dun?'

As usual it shows the influence of Poe, one of whose stories is based on a manuscript found in a bottle. Verne outdoes him by having *three* manuscripts, bearing the same message in English, French, and German. They are badly damaged by sea-water and the problem is to interpret their combined information.

The bottle is found in the stomach of a shark caught by the crew of a steam yacht owned by a wealthy Scots laird, Lord Glenarvan; the influence of Scott is obvious here. Even when the documents are translated and correlated, their message is still incomplete: Captain Grant and two of his seamen have been cast ashore and are pleading for help.

After getting into touch with the Captain's two children, Glenarvan is urged by his kind-hearted wife to go to the rescue in his yacht. The difficulty is to know where to go: the message gives the latitude of the place where the castaways were wrecked, but the longitude has been obliterated and its wording is ambiguous. Glenarvan decides to make for the most likely place and to follow the given parallel of latitude either until the castaways are reached or until all hope has to be abandoned.

Hardly is the yacht out at sea when she is found to be carrying an involuntary castaway. This is the French geographer Paganel, as notorious for his absent-mindedness as he is famous for his erudition.

As his knowledge may be helpful and he is companionable, he forms a welcome reinforcement to the expedition and he confirms their tentative reading of the message.

The very length of the book shows that the castaways are not where they were expected, and the rescuers have to travel more than half-way round the world in search of them. They show unfailing resourcefulness and courage in the face of a multitude of perils, from flood and fire and earthquake, from natives and 'civilized' bandits, from the treachery of a seaman who claims to have definite knowledge of Captain Grant's fate. Their course is determined not only by fresh interpretations of the message but also by Papanel's absent-mindedness, and the surprise ending turns on a detail of geographical nomenclature that he had overlooked.

This detail is so obscure that even if armed, as would be essential, with a French atlas and gazetteer, the reader is hardly likely to solve the mystery. To give him a chance of doing so, here are the composite message and its French component, in which the essential clue is concealed. Failing this, where would he advise Lord Glenarvan to make for, and when the castaways are found not to be there, where should he make for next?

Troi ats tannia
gonie austral
abor
contin pr cruel indi
jété ongit
et 37° 11 lat

June 7th 1862 frigate *Britannia* Glasgow
went down gonie austral
by land two sailors
Captain Gr. land
contin. pr. cruel indi
throw this paper in longitude
and latitude 37° 11′ Take them help
lost

While writing this story Verne had undertaken another task; unwise though this was, he might have found it embarrassing to decline. When another of Hetzel's authors, Theophile Lavallée, had died while compiling an *Illustrated Geography of France*, it was only natural that the publisher should ask Verne to take over the work, and Verne could hardly refuse. He was, like his character Paganel, an 'armchair geographer', the work though exacting would be remunerative, and he was under an obligation to Hetzel, who had given him his start. He made the book, as one would expect, remarkable for its precision and clearness.[1]

This exacting toil, which demanded several journeys about France, told on Verne, who had never quite recovered from the struggles and privations of his earlier days. His headaches returned and brought on attacks of ill-temper; he snapped at the children, refused invitations to go out shooting, and was surly to well-meaning admirers who sought only to congratulate him. 'I'll never venture again', said one of them ruefully, 'to stroke that polar bear.' It seems a pity he did not know our expression, 'a bear with a sore head'.

No sooner had Verne finished the *Geography* than he decided to leave Paris; the call of the sea had never stopped sounding in his ears, and here was a chance to respond to it. Le Crotoy, at the mouth of the Somme, was then a small fishing village. Here, early in 1866, he rented a house on the shore, where he could work within the sound of the waves; here, now that he was working on his second moon-flight story and contemplating a book tentatively entitled *Voyage beneath the Oceans*, he might well hope for inspiration.

Honorine was not enthusiastic; though the weather at Le Crotoy was good, the winds were cold and the place seemed right off the map. By now, however, she was used to the vagaries of the artistic temperament, and she knew that if it came to withstanding her erratic husband when he was in the throes of inspiration she might as well try to resist one of the forces of nature. And if the sea air and the loneliness were to restore his health the inconvenience would be worth while.

Her two daughters were even less enthusiastic and longed to be back with their friends in their Parisian boarding-school, but in those days teenagers knew their place. Apart from Jules himself, probably the only one in the Verne family to enjoy the move was his small son

[1] René Escaich.

Michel, and even he was scared at the small popgun of a cannon at the prow of his father's boat—and with good reason, too, for the crew never fired it without commending their souls to God, and at last, when firing a salute, it exploded![1]

This boat, the *St Michel*, was one of the local eight-ton fishing-craft that specialized in shrimping, and Verne had adapted her for pleasure cruising. She had a forecastle for her crew and a small cabin in her stern for her skipper and his guests, a cubby-hole, measuring ten feet by five and only four and a half feet high. Apart from such amenities as two bunks and three seaweed mattresses, described as of 'relative softness', its chief article of furniture was its cupboard, holding not only the charts and tide-tables indispensable to navigation, but above all the reference books indispensable to her owner's work.

Like Michel Ardan in the space-capsule, Verne was no mere passenger. Dressed as a seaman,[2] he took his share in the boat's handling, though he always confided this to his crew in moments of peril. Soon he was delighted to find that 'breath of sea air cures the neuralgia which the breath of inspiration throws in my face'.[3]

The two fishermen who formed his crew adored him, but they said disappointedly that 'M'sieur Verne knows nothing about fishing, he cares for the fish only when it's on the end of his fork'. They declared that he seemed to cast a spell over the fish: whereas normally they could take a good catch with only a bit of pipe-stem as bait, when he was aboard they got nothing even if they baited with truffles. He used to chaff them about this, and one day they began to chaff him, for they caught a fine mackerel—until as they were taking it off the hook it wriggled out of their grasp and bounced from the boat's side back into the sea!

What they did not realize, to use an expression which would have delighted that inveterate punster Jules Verne, was that he had other fish to fry. As, after lending a hand with the sails or doing duty at the helm, he lay sprawled face-downwards on the deck, he was 'fishing' in his imagination for the monsters of the deep or visualizing the heavens as seen from beyond the air. 'How do you manage

[1] Jules Claretie, *Jules Verne*.

[2] It was probably at this time that, realizing the difficulties of using a 'cut-throat' razor at sea, Verne, hitherto clean-shaven, grew his chestnut beard.

[3] Jules Claretie.

to write such beautiful things about the sky,' Honorine wanted to know, 'when you only look at it with the seat of your pants?'

His work on the *Geography* enabled him to take a badly needed holiday. When he had seen the *Great Eastern* during his visit to Britain he had vowed to cross the Atlantic in her, and now was his chance to do so.

The record of this unfortunate vessel, meant to be the triumph of her age and the masterpiece of her inventor, Brunel, is as fantastic as the strangest of Verne's *Strange Journeys*. By far the largest ship to be built until quite recent times, she was too massive for her own engines. Apart from that inherent defect she seemed fated throughout her career; from her repeated refusal to be launched and the fatal accident which distressed Brunel's dying moments, to her ignominious end as the floating advertisement of a department-store, she might have been under a curse.[1]

Her evil reputation was not likely to deter Jules Verne, and she had somewhat redeemed it by successfully laying a transatlantic cable. Its first message, from President Andrew Johnson to Queen Victoria, ran: 'Glory to God in the highest and peace on earth to men of goodwill.'

Nothing could have pleased Verne more, for he was an enthusiast for world peace, and, in his rather optimistic opinion: 'To be able to live in continual communication with all humanity would clear up many misunderstandings.'

In the spring of 1867 he and his brother Paul sailed in the *Great Eastern* from Liverpool to New York and back. While in America they visited the Niagara Falls, where the scenery, so reminiscent of Fenimore Cooper, led them to adopt the names of his two characters, Hawkeye and Chinganook. Greatly as he enjoyed the trip, Jules never forgot that he was a writer in search of copy; he chatted with the seamen who had helped to lay the cable and gathered material for use in his forthcoming story, now to be called *Voyage beneath the Waters*.

His account of the trip was not published until 1871. *A Floating City* is a queer mixture of reportage, improved or marred, according to taste, by some 'fine writing', with sheer romancing. After describing the vessel and summarizing her history, Verne recalls one of the fatalities which marked her career:

[1] James Dugan, *The Great Iron Ship*.

'So little do the Anglo-Saxons regard death that this event made little impression on board. These unhappy men, killed and wounded alike, were only tools, which could be replaced at very little expense.'

As a Roman Catholic he was sardonically amused at the Protestant Sabbath. Even the ship's bell, he declares, as it called the people to worship had 'a kind of solemn religious tone' unlike its usual metallic peal. The captain did not order the sails to be hoisted, as this would be 'improper', though the screw was kept at work. 'That which comes directly from God must be respected' was the unofficial explanation; 'the wind is in His hand, the steam is in the power of man'.

He was impressed when the captain led a reading from the Old Testament; this 'claimed the respect and attention of the most indifferent'. But when some American minister began what promised to be a long sermon, Verne just got up and walked out.

His description of a concert is more satirical; it was 'as good as amateur soirées generally are, chiefly a success for the performers and their friends'. The triumph of the evening was not on the programme: some Americans asked the pianist, Paul Verne, to play the French National Anthem. Apparently they failed to recognize the Imperial Anthem, *Partant pour la Syrie*, and clamoured for the real one. So Paul, 'with a compliance which betokened rather a musical facility than political convictions', delighted them with the *Marseillaise*.

The narrative includes some entertaining pen-pictures of the passengers, but in so composite a book one cannot be sure how far these are imaginary or factual. As for the fictional story woven into it, this is far too melodramatic to be taken seriously: Allott compares it to a Victorian novelette, but a reviewer in an American science fiction magazine thinks of it as almost prophetic:

'A plot that belongs in soap opera and was therefore ahead of its time . . . right out of afternoon T.V. or radio. Will the dashing Captain MacElwin regain his lost sweetheart? Is the madwoman in black the fair Ellen? Will her husband, the villainous international gambler Drake, force MacElwin into a duel and cut him down? If the captain kills the gambler, how can he ever

> marry the widow of the man he has slain? Will Ellen ever regain her sanity?'[1]

For the answers to these questions, and to find out how they arise, the reader is referred to the book. Absurd as the story is, however, it throws an interesting light on the conventions and outlook of the time.

A Floating City is on the short side. To eke it out, Hetzel included in the same volume a long-short story which Verne had contributed to the *Musée des Familles* in 1865. *The Blockade Runners* is a narrative of the American Civil War; while showing clearly where his own sympathies lay, he succeeds in making his hero delightfully impartial. By assisting Federals and Confederates at once, a captain brings his vessel simultaneously under fire from both sides, each enraged with him because he has assisted the other!

[1] *Astounding Science Fiction*, December 1957.

VII

'Freedom, Music, and the Sea'

GREATLY as Verne had enjoyed his trip across the Atlantic, from the stuffy Victorian comfort and elegance of the *Great Eastern* he returned with a sigh of relief to the austere simplicity of the *St Michel.* Refreshed by his holiday, he plunged with renewed energy into his work. 'As I write', he told his father, 'the sea is too strong for us to go out. But the *St Michel* is a floating study now, and I work better on board than on dry land.'

Discussing his submarine story with Hetzel, he wrote that the difficulty was to make totally improbable things seem probable, and that he hoped to be successful, but it would take much attention to style; some of its passages, indeed, would demand the eloquence of a Mme Sand. He meant to make it, he added, 'very strange, quite unexpected, and certainly what had never been done before. This is not so conceited as it sounds. I know it's original and I hope it's good, that's all.'[1]

So reluctant was he to tear himself away from his floating study that when he went to Paris to see his publisher he decided to sail her up the Seine. Honorine, who might have been looking forward to visiting the capital, was pardonably annoyed:

> 'Hardly here and Jules is gone again. He has taken it into his head to go to Paris in the *St Michel.* In this drought he'll probably get stuck on a sandbank. So much the worse for him. It will be a real lesson to him, for he simply can't stay still.'

He did not run aground, but with the river so low his boat had to arrive somewhat ingloriously towed by a tug. Then Verne had to run the gauntlet of a crowd of sightseers avid for a glimpse of him, and the drought made the journey back down the Seine more difficult even than that upstream.

His new story, the famous *Twenty Thousand Leagues under the Sea* (1870), has some claims to be his masterpiece. It delighted Hetzel,

[1] Parménie and de la Chapelle.

who persuaded Verne to sit for his portrait to the artist Edouard Riou, as a model for the character who forms the story's narrator: Professor Pierre Aronnax, of the Paris Museum of Natural History, resembles a clean-shaven Jules Verne.

The Professor begins by recalling a number of inexplicable incidents. A 'sea monster' had been sighted, moving with incredible speed and described as incredibly large. A vessel strikes an uncharted reef and another is struck by 'something sharp and penetrating' which punches a hole two yards across in her iron hull. Attempts are made to explain these incidents, but the idea that some sort of submarine is involved is dismissed as wildly improbable.

Consulted by the New York press, Aronnax attributes the damage to an immense narwhal: 'a sea-unicorn of colossal dimensions, armed with a spur like a frigate's ram' and moving at twenty miles an hour. So plausible is his theory that the U.S. Government invites him to join an expedition sent out not only to find the monster but to rid the seas of it.

Embarking with his Flemish servant, Conseil, the Professor finds a congenial companion in 'the prince of harpooners'; a French-Canadian, Ned Land is a man not only of great technical skill but of intelligence and integrity. He it is who after a long period of fruitless search finds 'the thing' in the North Pacific. The light it emits suggests that it is akin to the 'torpedo fish' or electric ray; it spurts out great jets of air and water; its noises resemble breathing and the strokes of an immense tail. It can outspeed the American warship, whose shells merely glide off its thick rounded skin.

When Ned Land hurls his harpoon, 'a terrible weapon in his hands', the monster retaliates and Aronnax is hurled overboard, Conseil thinking it only natural to follow him. Almost on the verge of drowning they reach some floating object; upon it is Land, for he too had been flung into the sea. They are, he explains, actually upon the supposed narwhal; no wonder shells and harpoons were ineffective, for the creature is plated with sheet iron.

It is, in fact, a gigantic submarine, and almost at once she begins to submerge. . . .

While Verne did not, as is sometimes thought, 'invent' the submarine, he saw the possibilities of the pioneer underwater craft, crude and unreliable as they were. It was not so long ago that a French inventor had perished in such a vessel off Le Crotoy; and though it was an American who years ago had built the first practicable submarine, it was in French waters that he had sailed her. He had offered her to Napoleon, who however had declined her without thanks. Verne must often have mused on the effects of his country's naval history had she adopted Robert Fulton's two inventions, his submarine and his steam-boat.

Fulton's vessel had been called the *Nautilus*, and it was only natural that Verne should adopt this name for his fictional super-submarine. Her master, Captain Nemo, who is also her designer and builder, takes the three castaways on board and accepts them, with some reservations, as his guests. As enigmatic a figure as his name suggests, he is endowed with boundless arrogance and a wonderful gift for justifying himself.

Although he could not possibly have known anything about the American vessel until the survivors told him, and although he could have evaded her quite easily by submerging instead of attacking her, he denounces her action in hunting him all over the seas. 'I have done with society', he declares when Aronnax protests, 'for reasons which I alone can understand'—and which remain unexplained throughout the story.

On compassionate grounds, however, he consents to keep them on board for life, subject to their agreeing to be immured in their cabins whenever he wishes. 'In thus acting I exonerate you completely, for I make it impossible for you to see what you ought not to see.'

Disquieted though he feels, Aronnax is tempted by this unique opportunity of research into his subject, marine biology, from a 'floating study' within the ocean depths. Insisting that no word of honour precludes him from escaping, he agrees, whereupon Nemo unbends and shows him over his ship.

She is certainly worth a visit. Her library contains twelve thousand volumes, and her saloon, aptly described by Allott as a 'Sam Goldwyn nightmare', is both a natural history museum and an art gallery; its contents range from unique biological specimens to masterpieces of painting and sculpture, and a piano-organ is strewn with the works of the greatest composers.

In contrast with this, and with the elegance of the cabin assigned to Aronnax, Nemo's own quarters are as simply furnished as a monastic cell. The difference is even more striking than that between the amenities of the *Great Eastern* and Verne's little cubby-hole on the *St Michel.*

Nemo shows Aronnax the submarine's control-room and discusses her motive-power somewhat cryptically. 'Professor,' he announces portentously, 'my electricity is not everybody's electricity, and you will permit me to withhold further details.'

The *Nautilus,* he explains, is over two hundred feet long and her maximum breadth is twenty-five feet; her outer hull is streamlined to reduce water resistance. She is propelled by screws and steered horizontally by a rudder; she submerges and surfaces either by using hydroplanes like horizontal rudders or by filling and emptying her tanks. The helmsman is housed in a conning-tower fitted with glass lenses ten inches thick, and another similar superstructure contains a powerful searchlight.

Her water-tight boat can be launched even when she is submerged; though propelled not electrically but by sails or oars, it is connected to the parent vessel by an electric cable. An air-lock and self-contained diving-dresses enable captain and crew to go out hunting on the sea-floor, their magazine air-guns firing electric bullets giving a lethal shock.

Their equipment also enables them to attend the burial of a fallen comrade. The funeral service has already been held on board, and after the body has been lowered into its coral grave, Captain Nemo and his crew kneel in silent prayer, while the Professor and his two companions bow reverently.

' "Your dead sleep peacefully," Aronnax tries to console him. "Out of the reach of sharks."

' "Yes, sir," the captain replies gravely. "Of sharks and men." '

The burial follows an episode which Aronnax found disquieting. He was on deck and had raised his telescope to scan the horizon when it was snatched out of his hands:

> 'I turned. Captain Nemo was before me but I could hardly recognize him. His face was transfigured. His eyes flashed angrily; his teeth were set; his taut body, clenched fists, his head hunched between his shoulders, betrayed the violent agitation which pervaded his whole frame.'

Without explanation he hustles his guests below and they are given a drugged meal. On his return to consciousness the Professor, a qualified medical man, is asked to treat one of the crew who had sustained terrible head injuries. Nothing can be done for him, and the captain is evasive, merely saying unconvincingly that the man was struck down as the result of some shock.

In spite of his enthusiasm for the *Nautilus* and the help she gives in his researches, Aronnax gets more and more uneasy, while Ned Land is being driven so frantic by this endless imprisonment that even the impassive Conseil becomes alarmed and watches him carefully, lest he do something desperate. The situation grows intolerable. . . .

Such episodes are brilliantly described in *Twenty Thousand Leagues*. Even in its unabridged form the story is not spoiled by the parenthetical disquisitions on marine biology, and with these omitted it teems with excitement: the *Nautilus* is repeatedly saved from fantastic perils only by her captain's resourcefulness and skill.

The sheer brilliance of the narrative overcomes defects that in a lesser work might well have been fatal. One is almost too big to be noticed; Verne himself may have overlooked it, or he may have felt that to take it into account would spoil the story.

Certainly he could not plead ignorance or inexperience. As a yachtsman he knew what in a choppy sea befalls objects not securely fixed down, and he had regaled his friends with a graphic account of the effects of an unexpected wave on the *Great Eastern*.

In this respect the submerged submarine is especially vulnerable:

> 'She rolls very easily; she is, of course, no heavier or lighter than the water in which she floats, and if by chance she touches bottom in shallow water she bounds about like a rubber ball on a pavement. . . . Inside, the sailors are thrown about and dashed against the machinery.[1]

Such troubles hardly affect the *Nautilus*. Among her varied exploits she runs aground; she is struck by a capsized iceberg and collides with others; she accidentally or deliberately rams some surface vessels; she twists and turns in pursuit of a school of cachalots and is smitten by their tails; above all, she submerges so deeply that on resurfacing, 'after having leaped into the air like a flying-fish she fell back, throwing up the waves to a tremendous height'.

[1] H. G. Wells, *The Undying Fire*.

Yet the sole result of these manoeuvres is that one member of her crew becomes a casualty—Verne apparently did not foresee the need for a safety-belt and a crash-helmet—and that on one occasion, and on one only, 'the furniture is thrown about'. Even after this an illustration shows that the suit of armour which figures in Captain Nemo's expensive collection of bric-à-brac is still erect on its pedestal!

To adapt the immortal words of Sherlock Holmes, I would also like to draw the reader's attention:

'To the curious incident of the crew in the sunshine.'

'The crew did nothing in the sunshine.'

'That is the curious incident.'

For the crew do next to nothing either in the sunshine or in the open air. The mate comes momentarily on deck every day to scan the horizon, Captain Nemo makes a longer stay to take his bearings or to expatiate to Aronnax on the glory and freedom of the sea. But his men are quite content to be cooped in their floating home even when she is surfaced, leaving her only for an occasion excursion in their diving-dresses across the sea-floor. So seldom are they mentioned that the story would need little alteration were the *Nautilus* 'manned' by robots or mechanized throughout.

On the other hand, Verne's depiction of his chief character is astonishingly vivid. Yet the book leaves some questions unanswered. Who is Captain Nemo, and what is his quarrel with humanity? What is the nationality of the vessel which he deliberately sinks? Possibly Verne had not yet thought these details out; or he may not have wished to alienate his British readers.

A later book makes it abundantly clear that Nemo's quarrel is not so much with mankind as with Britain. So cruelly had he been bereaved in the Indian Mutiny that whenever he encounters a vessel of the Royal Navy he feels justified in sinking her on sight. No wonder he honours the wreck of a certain vessel, for, after a glorious battle against odds, she had been sunk by the British during the Napoleonic wars; renowned in French naval history, she is *Le Vengeur*.

On gaining his vengeance he finds it turns to dust and ashes in his mouth. He had already sunk one ship, and then he was too preoccupied with his injured comrade to spare a thought for his victims. Now he is able to glut his eyes with their fate as he watches them dragged to their death with the sinking vessel. Horror-struck at

Jules Verne at twenty-five: photograph by Nadar

The 'Time Demon', from *Master Zacharius*

In free-fall, from *Round the Moon*

Jules Verne at the height of his career

the sight and overwhelmed with remorse, he falls on his knees before the portrait of his dead wife and children as though imploring their forgiveness.

By the end of his life, as the later book shows, Nemo, with his passion for self-justification, has managed to convince himself, in flat contradiction of the earlier narrative, that the vessel had deliberately trapped the *Nautilus* in a shallow inlet where she could neither escape nor submerge, so that he had been forced to sink her in self-defence.

After this tragedy his nerve increasingly fails. Now on the surface, now submerged, he steers at random northwards as though fleeing from the scene of his crime. 'Almighty God! Enough! Enough!' he murmurs, so oblivious of his course that he is trapped in a peril—derived from a story by Poe—from which escape seems impossible.

Aronnax and his two companions, who have chosen this very moment to escape, realize their danger only too late; whether they continue with their plan or seek to stay with the vessel, they seem equally doomed. . . .

There is more in the captain of the *Nautilus* than the thirst for vengeance; in some respects he is a personification of his creator. 'At heart,' declared Verne's nephew Maurice, 'my uncle Jules had only three passions: freedom, music and the sea'; Verne had in his youth written and composed a number of songs, mostly dealing with nautical subjects.

These were likewise the ruling passions of Nemo. Improvising on his organ, 'he touched only the black keys, which gave his melodies an essentially Scottish character'; in his agonies of conscience they became 'a sad harmony to an indefinable chant, the wail of a soul longing to break the bonds of earth'.

Nemo sympathizes, as did Verne, with revolts against tyranny; he subsidizes the Cretans, in their rising against the Turks, with treasures looted from a Spanish galleon sunk in Vigo Bay. Like Verne he loves the sea, not only for itself, but because it symbolizes all he values most:

> 'The sea is everything. Its breath is pure and healthy. Here man is never lonely, for on all sides he feels life astir. The sea does not belong to despots. Upon its surface men can still make unjust laws, fight, tear one another to pieces, wage wars of terrestrial

horror. But at thirty feet below their reign ceases, their influence is quenched, and their power disappears. Ah, sir, live—live in the bosom of the waters. There alone I recognize no master! There I am free!'

Unlike Nemo, however, Verne recognized a duty to society. It is not only in appearance that Aronnax resembles him, for he personifies other aspects of his character; both felt it incumbent on them to give their knowledge to the world.

Twenty Thousand Leagues, which appeared in 1870, was completed in 1868, only six years after Verne had started work on *Five Weeks in a Balloon.* In that short time, besides his share in a standard geographical work, he had written half a dozen of his *Strange Stories*: three exciting narratives of adventure and three classics of science fiction. He had created some memorable characters and devoted as much loving care to descriptions of the uncharted Polar Seas and the unknown heart of Africa, the unexplored depths of ocean and earth, and the then unattainable regions beyond the air, as the greatest novelists have lavished on the subtle details of character.

He had not only founded science fiction and its branch the space-travel story, he had shown that they are compatible with humour, with lucid prose, with brilliant characterization, and with a sincere religious faith.

Though during his long career as an author he produced many other splendid works, never again did he show such sustained creativeness. He might have done so but for an unforeseen event which had endless effects upon himself, his thought, his publishers, his public, and the world in which he lived.

VIII
Post-war Reconstruction

VERNE's delight in the appearance of his new books was quickly damped. *Round the Moon* and *Twenty Thousand Leagues* were both published in 1870: and in July of that year began the Franco-Prussian War.

Its outbreak evoked an epidemic of war-fever, but Verne never contracted this, He, who could foresee the dirigible balloon, the submarine and a giant cannon—larger even than the 'Big Bill' which the Germans had already constructed—could well imagine the possibilities of mechanized warfare, and he was under no illusions as to the German character. When someone talked about giving those Prussians a good hiding, he replied that he was not so anxious to give them a hiding, or, what was certainly possible, to see them give a hiding to the French.

Nor was he reassured on being made a Chevalier of the Legion of Honour; this was on the nomination of Ferdinand de Lesseps, about whose Suez Canal project Captain Nemo had waxed so enthusiastic. Empty as Verne may have felt such a tribute in war-time, it had one advantage that he did not realize till later; it took him to Chantenay, where his father wanted to 'celebrate', and this was the last time the two met.

Meanwhile Hetzel had reprinted the appropriate sections of the Lavallée-Verne *Geography*, those on the Départements between the frontier and Paris, in which military operations might be expected, under the title *From Paris to the Rhine*.[1]

While Jules was at Chantenay he was called up for war duty. Too old to serve in the line, he was, on the strength of his prowess as a yachtsman, instructed to organize a coastguard service in the Somme bay. So disturbed was the country that he had to make a detour through Normandy and Brittany to reach his post at Le Crotoy, where he assumed command of his little force, twelve veterans of the Crimean War, armed with three flintlocks and a cannon, as he put

[1] René Escaich.

it, 'about the size of a poodle'. The task was not exacting, but he had to take care not to go so far afield as Ostend; if Belgium were to enter the war it would be on the German side, and he would be interned.

Apart from his natural distress and anxiety on behalf of his war-smitten country, his chief concern was about his family. The rumours that the Prussians were pillaging the countryside were so disquieting that, feeling that Honorine and the children would be safer in a town, he sent them to her family at Amiens.

Their absence, like his enforced return to his 'floating study', enabled him to get on with his work. The result appeared in 1872 under the clumsy and uninformative title, *The Adventures of Three Englishmen and Three Russians in South Africa*; it would better have been called *Measuring a Meridian.*

Its plot is simple: the six heroes are sent to estimate the earth's circumference by measuring an arc of a meridian in the favourable conditions of the Kalahari desert, in South Africa. They meet with the appropriate perils and adventures, and humour arises from the absent-mindedness of the Russian mathematician so oblivious of his surroundings that he is too busy correcting an error in a logarithmic table to notice that he is almost literally in the jaws of death. Technical interest comes from the detailed account given of the surveyor's methods.

One episode shows the influence of the time. While the surveyors are at work, they learn that the Crimean War has broken out. What are they to do? Become mutually hostile and have as little to do with one another as their task allows? Or put science first and regard themselves as civilized Europeans united against the hostile natives? . . .

As this narrative was being written, the war dragged on. The Empire of Napoleon III collapsed and the Third Republic took its place. Paris was besieged but Verne, as he wrote to Hetzel—from whom he got two letters by balloon or pigeon post—still believed in a victory for France 'in a second Valmy'. The Germans were now in Amiens, but that did not keep him from visiting his family.

Even the end of the war did not bring peace. It left Paris in the throes of a civil conflict, the Commune, waged fiercely and followed by harsh reprisals. France was defeated, subjected to a heavy indemnity, and stripped of her two frontier provinces.

As a patriotic Frenchman, Verne shared in his country's humiliation and sorrow, feeling the devastation in Paris as 'lamentable'. He was suffering, too, from his own personal anxieties and griefs. The death of one of his best friends was followed by a yet more distressing bereavement, that of his father; austere though Pierre Verne might be, he had been considerate and kind and had shown a sympathetic interest in his son's work, and Jules felt his loss acutely.

As might be expected, book-production was almost at a standstill. Hetzel, whose printers had been out fighting in the Commune, had been hurt by the war both in profit and in soul and said that he did not know whether he was still in business or not. It looked as if his author might have to return to stockbroking.

Verne's state of mind, Kenneth Allott suggests, was symbolized in his next story, *The Fur Country* (1873). A trading post of the Hudson's Bay Company stands on what seems to be solid ground, but is really a sheet of sea-ice. This is part of the Canadian ice-cap and though it is strewn so thickly with detritus that a forest has grown upon it, there is nothing beneath it but the Arctic Ocean! Glacier-fashion, the ice-sheet has 'calved', and the whole post is adrift upon a gigantic ice-floe. The currents are inexorably carrying it southwards through the Bering Strait, and immense though the floe is it is doomed to melt piecemeal in the warmer water of the Pacific. . . .

Yet in the midst of his anxieties Verne had something to reassure him: *Twenty Thousand Leagues* had won him recognition in the literary world. He had refused to kow-tow to the French Academy in the hope of getting one of its awards; in 1872 this was given him spontaneously amidst tumultuous applause. Dr Fergusson, of *Five Weeks in a Balloon*, when he made his memorable address to the Royal Geographical Society, could hardly have received a more enthusiastic ovation.

Life in France was gradually returning to normal: once more people were reading, and Hetzel felt he might resume publishing. Verne, needless to say, had never stopped writing, and now he hit on an idea that promised well. It had nothing to do with science fiction or exploration: its plot demanded that its characters should seek to follow the beaten track.

Its idea did not come, as has been suggested, from the advertisement of some travel-agency but from an article in *Le Magasin Pittoresque*.[1] This had pointed out that the cutting of the Suez Canal

[1] René Escaich, quoting the son of one of Jules Verne's friends.

would allow a tour around the world to be made in less than three months, and gave a detailed itinerary showing how it could be accomplished in eighty days.

Such a journey would have a paradoxical effect upon real and apparent time which Poe had glanced at in a silly and badly written trifle, *Three Sundays in a week.* Seriously and competently written, here was a theme after Verne's own heart, with a surprise ending arising quite naturally out of the story. But whoever would want to tear about the world like that?

Verne imagined the most unlikely person possible. He makes the hero of *Around the World in Eighty Days* (1873) a phlegmatic Englishman, Phileas Fogg, whose whole life is a matter of routine. He engages a Frenchman, nicknamed Passepartout because he has been in and out of so many jobs, who is tired of his versatile career and anxious to settle down. The man had heard that Fogg was the most precise and sedentary man in Britain, and in his service he might forget the very word 'Passepartout'.

'Passepartout suits me,' Fogg tells him. 'You are engaged.'

Then, that very evening, Passepartout is amazed to be told to pack his master's kit and his own: they are about to set out on a tour of the world.

Getting useful background material from an article, *The English at Home,* in the *Musée des Familles,* Verne describes an evening's whist at the Reform Club. During the game a mention of a recent bank robbery leads the players into an argument about the speed of modern travel. Is it really possible, as the papers declare, to travel round the world in eighty days?

Fogg maintains that it is, and wagers £20,000 that he would return in the given time, to the minute, with his passport duly stamped to show that he had accomplished his task. That sum was half his entire fortune; the rest would defray his expenses.

Hardly has he started when he is in danger of arrest. Fix, a detective, suspects him of being a bank-robber and his tour a mere pretext for fleeing the country. As no arrest can be made until a warrant arrives, Fix, masquerading as a helpful fellow-traveller, does his utmost to delay Passepartout and Fogg.

Serialized in the Paris *Temps,* the journey attracted in real life almost as much attention as it did in the story. Seeing the possibilities of advertisement, some of the leading steamship companies offered to pay for having one of their vessels used to enable Fogg to complete his journey across the Atlantic. To Verne such an arrangement was unworthy of a literary man, and he found his own way of bringing Fogg back to England, only to be arrested by his false friend the detective Fix. . . .

Hetzel may have dropped Verne a hint that readers appreciate a love interest, for the story includes a charming heroine whom Fogg, aided by the versatile Passepartout, finds time to rescue from an appalling death.

Such a story clamoured to be put on the stage, just as in recent times it clamoured to be put on the screen. The dramatist Adolphe d'Ennery, who adapted it, made as free with the plot and sought spectacular effects as regardless of expense as any modern film-producer.

Not content with such scenes as a funeral pyre and a train attacked by Red Indians, d'Ennery added, among others, the masthead of a sunken ship and a snake-infested cave in Malaya—the stage-directions optimistically demanded 'hundreds' of serpents! For contemporary notions of propriety he introduced a second heroine, so that the two could chaperone one another. This of course demanded a subsidiary hero, and he, with a view to visitors from across the Atlantic, was made an American. Passepartout was given a sweetheart, thus affording an opportunity for a touch—but no more than a touch—of the sauciness without which, some visitors from abroad might think, no Parisian stage-show could possibly be complete.

Verne's opinion of this mangling of his work may be inferred from one of his comments. Having during the recent siege slaughtered and devoured all the inmates of their zoo, as well as their pets and the very rats from the sewers, the Parisians were avid for the sight of animals. One in particular delighted them: 'the trumpeter of my fame', Verne called it. 'The first half of the evening', he remarked ironically, 'the audience are longing for the elephant to appear, and the rest of the evening they are regretting that they won't see it again!'

He found no consolation in the varied correspondence the play evoked, ranging from begging letters and requests for locks of his hair to proposals of marriage. On the other hand, his financial troubles were at an end. 'The play isn't a success,' the producer assured him, 'it's a fortune.' His publisher Hetzel also shared the reward indirectly, for the play gave Verne widespread publicity and helped the sale of his books. Realizing what he owed to his author, he several times modified their contract to the latter's benefit.

At his wife's request, Verne now decided to leave Paris and to settle down in Amiens, a friendly cultured city where he was welcomed by a cordial and well-read circle of friends, and where he was conveniently near to the capital though far enough away for him not to be affected by its bustle and din. About the same time he indulged himself in a luxury: he replaced his converted fishing-smack by a small sailing yacht, the *St Michel II*, in which his family as well as himself might enjoy an occasional cruise.

In more recent times Verne's story has been dramatized in Britain, not with such spectacular effects as by d'Ennery, but with quite as many liberties. In one version it was given a novel twist. An English revue, *Round in Fifty*, showed Fogg, now an old man, as ordering a grandson—represented by George Robey—to go round the world in fifty days. As in the original story, the travellers think they have returned too late, but in the revue the situation is saved by an ingenious use of Summer Time![1]

The latest development (1963) has been an adaptation of *Around the World in Eighty Days* on ice! As this is based not on the book of that name but on a spectacular film based upon it—or possibly on a 'stage musical' based on that film—a cynic might say that any resemblance between the ice-show and Verne's narrative is likely to be purely coincidental.

[1] George Robey, *Looking Back on Life*.

IX

'It's Strogoff!'

VERNE'S reputation was now so great that Hetzel felt that the time was ripe to revive some of his earlier works. As the next of his stories, *Doctor Ox*, was too short to make a book, in 1874 he included with it three reprints from the *Musée*: *Master Zacharius, A Drama in the Air*, and *A Winter amid the Ice*. Then, for good measure, he added Paul Verne's account of his adventures during *The Fortieth French Ascent of Mont Blanc*.

Jules Verne, a professional author, was an amateur seaman; his brother Paul, a professional seaman, was an amateur author, and Jules occasionally gratified him by getting one of his efforts into print. *The Ascent* makes almost as laborious reading as its title suggests, and it would hardly interest modern mountaineers.

The scene of *Doctor Ox* is an imaginary Flemish town, whose people are so stolid that nobody in it ever moves quickly or makes an avoidable decision, and where all courtships last ten years. The mysterious doctor undertakes to light the town with 'oxyhydric gas' at his own expense; he instals the pipes, but there is a delay in fixing the burners.

Then strange unheard-of things happen. Some of the townsfolk actually 'talk politics'; an opera, normally performed so slowly that it takes four evenings, is rushed through with incredible speed; a dignified ball ends in a wild gallop.

Plants grow stupendously; shrubs become trees, the corn ripens in a few days, 'the cabbages are bushes and the mushrooms umbrellas'; pears take four men to eat them; and a tulip is large enough to hold a bird's nest. Then the plants fade as fast as they have grown.

The domestic animals, hitherto docile, turn restive. Crime flourishes and the teenagers threaten to become juvenile delinquents. A marriage takes place after only a few months' courtship.

Finally, just as the citizens have mustered an army and are about to launch an attack upon a neighbouring township, there is a terrific explosion. The gas works have blown up; when the smoke clears away Dr Ox and his assistant have vanished, and life at once returns to normal.

The mystery surrounding these strange events is hinted at in the story's title, and Verne had forecast it in a passage in *Round the Moon.* He treats the idea so lightly that it was turned into a musical comedy, in 1877, by Offenbach and Philippe Gilles. Yet, whether he realized this or not, it has serious implications, the possibility that a community's whole outlook and way of life may be transformed by an unscrupulous central agent. In the citizens of that imaginary Flemish town is a hint of the 'admass' of today.

Hetzel's decision to revive those earlier stories may have given Verne the idea of showing him the beginning of a yarn he had written in 1861 but never completed. *Uncle Robinson* opens with a mutiny and a refugee family landing on an uninhabited island. In spite of a volcano, an intelligent dog, a tractable ape, a resourceful French sailor, the 'Uncle Robinson' of the title, and the mysterious finding of a bullet in a piece of meat, the story had petered inconclusively out.

Hetzel rejected it with furious annotations. 'Where's the science? . . . It's too silly! . . . 82 pages of MS and nothing an absolute idiot wouldn't have thought of! . . . Your other characters have all been alive, but here they're all languid! . . . Cut it down by half and buck it up! . . .'[1]

Far from being offended, Verne acted on this advice. He found the science by studying chemistry and visiting a chemical works, warning Hetzel cheerfully that he would charge him for the acid stains on his clothing, but declaring that the revised story was going on like a house on fire ('*comme sur des roulettes*').[2]

And so, indeed, it was. In *The Mysterious Island* trilogy (1875), the 'languid' refugee family have been replaced by five energetic Americans, all sympathizers with the North during the American Civil War, who escape in a balloon from internment by the Southerners. Blown far across the Pacific by a gale, they land on a desert island. Less fortunate than Verne's favourite heroes 'the Robinsons', who had the whole cargo of a wrecked ship at their

[1] Jean H. Guermonprez, 'Une Oeuvre Inconnue de Jules Verne' (in *Livres de France: Revue Littéraire Mensuelle*, May/June 1955).

[2] Parménie and de la Chapelle.

disposal, these castaways have little more than the clothes they stand up in: only a match, two watches, the metal collar of their dog, and a solitary grain of wheat.

Yet they outdo even Robinson Crusoe by taking the bearings of their island and setting up a pottery, an iron-foundry, and a munition works. They blast a fortified home out of the solid rock. They cultivate the ground and produce a cornfield and a vegetable garden; they domesticate the birds and beasts and train a docile ape as their servant. They build a sailing-boat and lay a telegraph line to keep in touch with their corral. In short they mechanize the whole island and look forward to making it the thirty-eighth state of their Union. The reader would not be surprised if they were to design a 'flying machine', return to America, and win the war for the North by bombing the Southern armies.

Instead they receive inexplicable help; their unconscious leader is rescued from drowning by an unknown hand, and among other acts of beneficence is the arrival from nowhere of a chest containing everything, including a Bible, that castaways could possibly want.

When a floating bottle brings tidings that there is another castaway on a neighbouring island, these super-Robinsons go to his rescue. They find a dangerous madman, driven insane by sheer loneliness; when restored to sanity he is so overcome by remorse for a misspent life that he shuns their society. At last he confesses who he is.

Here there is a 'hark back' to Verne's earlier story, *The Children of Captain Grant*, for the castaway is a mutineer and would-be pirate whom Lord Glenarvan had marooned on that desert island. Repentant now, he helps the castaways resist an attack by his former comrades the pirates.

Again comes that mysterious help: the pirate ship inexplicably blows up and the pirates are slain by some incomprehensible weapon. At last a message arrives from some anonymous telegraphist, instructing the recipients to follow a wire they themselves had not laid. It then leads to a cavern where a submarine is afloat.

The reader will have no difficulty in guessing who the unknown benefactor is. Just as the marooned seaman tied up an end left loose in *The Children of Captain Grant*, so *The Secret of the Island* (as volume three of the trilogy was called) ties up the loose end of the finest of Verne's works. (And though its details are inconsistent with that earlier narrative, this does not spoil the story.)

Fascinating in itself, the trilogy shows that though in theory Verne loved the idea of life on an uninhabited island, he had no illusions about its effects in practice. Solitude had degraded a man—the marooned seaman—almost into a beast; association with benevolent human beings had turned a beast—the tractable ape—almost into a man.[1] The mere sight of comradeship and co-operation had given an embittered misanthrope renewed faith in human nature and converted him into a benevolent friend.

In the same year (1875) appeared the grimmest story Verne wrote. Apart from the obvious influence of Poe, *The Chancellor* is said to have three sources: the tragic voyage of the *Sarah Sands* in 1857; a painting, *The Wreck of the 'Medusa'*, by the French artist J. L. A. Theodore Gericault; and Captain Bligh's open-boat voyage after the mutiny on the *Bounty*.[2]

Whatever the story's origin, it certainly gave Verne a chance to let himself go. He belabours the unfortunate *Chancellor* with almost everything he can think of, short of a direct hit from a meteorite. The nervous breakdown of her captain, just after she leaves port, is followed by a succession of perils: fire down below, with smuggled explosives in the hold; a gale; imprisonment in an inland lagoon; and impending mutiny among the crew.

Finally, when her famished survivors are contemplating the last dreadful resort, they meet with an unexpected difficulty, a conscientious objector to cannibalism. Horrified when they propose to eat the body of someone dead from natural causes, he surreptitiously throws it overboard, with the natural result, which he ought to have foreseen, that they decide to kill and eat someone else. . . .

Normally averse from society, Verne, in 1877, decided to hold a large-scale fancy-dress ball, issuing eight hundred invitations. The work this involved proved too much for Honorine, who had not fully recovered from a serious illness, and she was in such danger that, as a desperate last resort, a blood-transfusion was ordered.

'Now', commented Verne, 'came an event unique in human history, a man offering his blood to save his mother-in-law.' The blood-donor was the husband of Honorine's daughter Suzanne, and the latter took over the duty of presiding over the ball.

Fortunately the blood-groups were compatible, and blood-trans-

[1] Gamarra: 'Jules Verne ou le Printemps', in *Europe*, April/May 1955.

[2] George H. Waltz, *Jules Verne: The Biography of an Imagination*.

fusion and ball were a success, Honorine making a complete recovery and enjoying the festivities from a distance. Its characters included the conventional Punch and Village Policemen, but the success of the evening was the emergence of the three spacemen from the projectile in *Round the Moon*!

Verne may have meant this jollification to celebrate the publication of another of his masterpieces, not space-travel but a story of adventure. Remembering the success of *Around the World*, he had written it with one eye on the stage.

Remembering also the liberties which d'Ennery had taken with that earlier production, he approached the impresario Felix Duquesnel, with a view to collaboration. Duquesnel refused, however, on the grounds that he was too lazy, and sent him back to d'Ennery, who, he said, would be certain to make a success of it.

The scene of this story is Russia, where Verne's books, translated by Mme Markovitch, had been warmly welcomed; he got the necessary local colour from the anarchist-prince Kropotkin through the intermediacy of Nadar's friend, the anarchist-geographer Elisée Réclus. Soon, as he told Hetzel, he was carried away writing it; he could think of nothing else.

Not unreasonably considering one episode unlikely, Hetzel consulted the Russian novelist Turgenev, who agreed, but added 'Never mind, it's a good story.' Lest it should give offence to the Russian authorities, their Ambassador in Paris, Prince Orloff, had also to be consulted. He simply advised a change of title, and the erstwhile *Courier of the Czar* accordingly appeared in 1876 as *Michel Strogoff*.[1] It sold well in Russia, as everywhere else.

Strogoff, a man of staunch loyalty and indomitable will, is sent by the Czar of Russia with urgent despatches to his brother, the Grand Duke, at Irkutsk, in Siberia. He faces dreadful perils, not only from storm and flood and wild beast but also from man, for the Tartars have invaded the country and he must pass between their lines. Nothing makes him swerve from his duty, even though he has to brand himself as a coward by refusing to retaliate, lest this delay him, when dealt a blow; even though he has to deny his own mother lest she reveal his identity. Captured by the Tartars, he is sentenced to an atrocious punishment.

The story has everything its reader—or a dramatist—could ask

[1] Parménie and de la Chapelle.

for: an ideal hero and a charming heroine; a detestable villain and a seductive 'vamp'; melodramatic situations; exotic scenery and costumes; a spectacular display of Oriental dancers and Tartar warriors; mother-love and the chiming of wedding bells. Humour is derived from two rival journalists, French and English.

It would hardly be thought that anything else would be needed for dramatic purposes, but d'Ennery added further attractions, including a performance by the Russian Ballet and a torchlight tattoo by the Czar's crack troops. He made more of the two journalists and delighted his audience with the Englishman's atrocious French accent.

All this took some time, and the play was not produced until 1880, after preliminary publicity suggestive of the modern Hollywood ballyhoo about yet another 'greatest picture of all time'.

Compared with these advance trumpetings, the play might well have disappointed public expectations, but it more than satisfied them. It became a sort of touchstone whereby other achievements could be judged, so that for some time the highest commendation of anything was expressed in the simple words 'It's Strogoff!'[1]

Devoid of factual basis, the narrative shows Verne's uncanny power of foresight. The imaginary Tartar invasion, 'futile as all attacks on the Russians Colossus must be', is foiled, as the real invasions of Napoleon and Hitler were foiled, by a drastic scorched earth policy, aided by 'General Winter'.

[1] Mme Allotte de la Fuÿe.

X
Tall Stories

NOW THAT Verne was being lionized he found that the process had its disadvantages; he was pestered with well-meaning admirers and had he been responsive he could have collected 'fans' like a modern pop-singer or television 'personality'.

Instead, he not merely snubbed and discouraged the lion-hunters, he treated even serious congratulations on his work with downright boorishness, and, as he himself admitted, his dour silence had the knack of putting an end to the conversation. His one desire was to get on with his work, but, failing to realize this, some busybodies sought for other motives for his aloofness.

Among them were cranks, one of whom, in 1875, told him portentously that his secret had been discovered. Jules Verne, the unknown visitor declared, was not a Frenchman at all but a Polish Jew who had renounced his faith to marry a Polish heiress, and though the engagement had been broken off he was still trying to conceal his Hebraic origin.

Verne, unfortunately, failed to realize how gossip spreads and how how even the wildest fabrications can gain credence. Instead of glancing at the alleged evidence for this nonsense, refuting it, and denying the story once and for all, he capped it with a better one. He added, speaking in serious tones but with his tongue in his cheek, that he had abducted the heiress; but his coldness had driven her to suicide and he was now suffering agonies of remorse. Beseeching his visitor to keep the matter dark, he went off to laugh over the joke.

He soon found that it was far from being a joke, for his visitor did nothing of the kind. Here was his story, actually confirmed by Verne himself, so that he need have no hesitation in spreading it far and wide. More or less embroidered, it cropped up intermittently, to its victim's intense annoyance, throughout his lifetime, and it even outlived him.

In 1939 Verne's Italian biographer, Edmondo Marcucci, was able to show its origin: there had been a Polish Jew who had taken the name of Julian de Verne, and the coincidence has made somebody jump to conclusions.[1] The antiquarian of Nantes, who had also gone thoroughly into the question, had likewise come to the not very surprising conclusion that Jules Verne really was Jules Verne.

Verne's annoyance at this story may account for his introduction into one of his next stories, *Hector Servadac* (1877), of a dishonest and avaricious Jewish pedlar. In America this was regarded as anti-Semitism; in one translation the pedlar's character was incredibly rehabilitated at the end of the story: in another his race was not mentioned and he was vaguely described as a Levantine.

The story itself is so remarkable that it cannot be summarized without revealing its secret and spoiling its whole effect. Its hero Servadac, a French officer resembling Verne's relative Captain Georges Allotte de la Fuÿe, is in a hut near the Algerian coast with his orderly Ben Zoof when they are knocked unconscious by some inexplicable cataclysm.

On their recovery they find that the laws of nature seem to have been altered; except that their immediate surroundings show little change, they might be living in a different world. Water boils at a surprisingly low temperature; the objects round them have become inexplicably light, as indeed have their own bodies, so that they can perform remarkable feats of high jumping. The very heavens are transformed, the sun travelling swiftly the wrong way across the sky; at night the Pointers no longer indicate the north; what looks like the moon seems to have a tiny moon of its own.

As the story progresses the incidents multiply, and the explanation, which it comes, is as remarkable as they are themselves. Yet it is the reverse of convincing, and the later part of the story lags into dullness. Verne tried to enliven it not only by cheap humour at the expense of the Jewish pedlar but by poking fun at the starchiness of some British officers and the cantankerous pedantry of a French astronomer.

There are some significant plays on words which seem more than the Vernian addition to puns. One is macabre, as the reader will see by simply reading the name 'Servadac' backwards. 'Ben Zoof' is said to mean 'Son of Wisdom' and Timaschoff (the name of a Russian Count who also figures in the narrative) 'Changing Time'.[2] Even

[1] E. Marcucci, *Giulio Verne e la sua Opera.*

[2] S. André Payre, 'Une Énigme de Jules Verne', in *Marsyas.*

relatively has been unconvincingly invoked to explain the story.

Perhaps a few words exchanged between two of the characters best sum things up:

'"Perhaps it isn't true, all the same!" suggested Ben Zoof.

'"Hang it all, I shall end up by believing it!" replied Captain Servadac.'

Financial success enabled Verne to escape the penalties of fame by the purchase, in 1876, of a larger yacht, the *St Michel III*, a combined sail-and-steamship which delighted him and won the judicious approval of his seafaring brother Paul Verne. Upon her he could take his family for a luxury cruise, gathering local colour as he went; upon her he would be safe from the lion-hunters and rumour-mongers who pursued him on land; and upon her he could stand on the bridge beside her captain, give a hand with the ropes, or do a trick at the wheel.

Her purchase recalled his first cruise, when he had visited Scotland and mourned over the desolation of an abandoned coal-mine. *Black Diamonds* (1877) opens with an affecting account of the closure of a mine, apparently exhausted—until, ten years later, its former overman invites its former engineer to revisit it. Though the invitation is anonymously countermanded almost at once, he accepts it, to learn that the overman, who with his wife and son has been living actually *within* the mine, has found indications of another seam.

A seam? It is an immense cavern from which extend seams of unparalleled richness. But its discoverers' lives are threatened: some malignant hand entombs them, while the flapping of invisible wings extinguishes their light. They would have perished had not some beneficent presence guided a rescue party to them.

Not merely are the new seams exploited; a whole town is built in the gigantic cavern, and some of the earlier mysteries are explained when a girl is found lying unconscious at the foot of a chasm leading to unexplored depths below. She could, but will not, explain the malignant presence which threatens the whole mine, and whose efforts to flood it destroy one of the finest of Scotland's beauty-spots. . . .

In 1878 a new influence appears in Verne's work; he had discovered Charles Dickens, whom he regarded as the 'master' of English writers, superior even to Stevenson and Captain Marryat.[1] *Bleak*

[1] Marie A. Belloc, 'Jules Verne at Home', in the *Strand Magazine*.

House especially impressed him, as is shown by his two next books.

The plot of *The Boy Captain* (1878) is suggested by its title: a youth of sixteen finds himself the only seaman on a passenger-carrying merchant-ship. Unfortunately, she carries a saboteur through whose machinations she is wrecked on the African coast, and all on board fall into the hands of a savage native king so debauched by unscrupulous white traders that his whole body is impregnated with alcohol. When someone suggests that it is worthy of so great a monarch to copy the white men by sampling some flaming brandy, he simply catches fire and dies, if not of spontaneous combustion, at any rate of something like it!

Apart from these 'fireworks', *The Boy Captain* is rather a humdrum story. This accusation cannot be raised against another which shows Verne's interest in town-planning, *The Begum's Fortune* (1879). A French authority on hygiene, Dr Sarrasin, is amazed to learn that, thanks to the fortunate marriage of a kinsman in India, he has inherited the wealth which gives the story its title.

Almost at once another claimant to the fortune appears, a German professor of chemistry. Verne's delayed reactions to the Franco-Prussian War are evident here, for Professor Schultz is the reverse of the irascible but good-hearted Lidenbrock; a sinister war-lord, he regards the Germans as a master-race whose mission it is to conquer the world.

His claim to the fortune is doubtful, but a firm of solicitors take it up and they, like Dr Sarrasin's legal advisers, look forward to a second 'Jarndyce and Jarndyce'. It is settled out of court, and though a cool million has been swallowed up in legal fees, the claimants are to divide twenty million pounds between them.

Each has his own use for the money. Sarrasin carries out a mammoth experiment in town-planning; his city, Frankville in Oregon, is designed on almost painfully hygienic principles. Very different is Stahlstadt, built thirty miles away by Schultz: it is little more than a self-contained munition factory, and is run on military lines with its own secret police.

Suspicions of its purpose, an Alsatian, Max Bruckman, enrols in its service and becomes its ruler's crony and confidential adviser. At last he learns its secret: it is the centre from which Schultz means to rule the world, his first step being to destroy Frankville. With a mammoth cannon of unprecedented range, he threatens to hurl upon the unsuspecting city missiles then unheard of but which have since been used with deadly effect in the two World Wars. And Max, the only man who knows his secret, is to pay for his knowledge with his life!

The super-cannon is fired, but Schultz has made a serious error. So great is the velocity he gives his missiles that it escapes from the earth's gravity, and 'endows the planetary world with a new star and the earth with a second satellite'!

Though not the first forecast of an artificial satellite—E. E. Hale's *The Brick Moon* antedated it by ten years[1]—this is certainly one of the earliest. It has the same technical defect as Verne's 'Moon' stories; the missile would be crushed and volatilized at the moment of discharge. Even if it did survive, moreover, its orbit would bring it back into the atmosphere, whose friction would slow it up and bring it down to earth.

Verne, however, showed foresight not only in Schultz's proposed weapons, but in the counter-measures adopted by Frankville. Civil Defence and fire-fighting services are organized, and preparations made for a mass evacuation of the women and children.

On learning that his attack has failed, Schultz decides to intensify it and to make Frankville 'a city of the dead without a surviving inhabitant . . . a modern Pompeii, at once a terror and a wonder to the whole world . . .'.

Verne plainly foresaw grim possibilities in the Teutonic character, and these were only too clearly realized when 'German' became almost a synonym for 'frightfulness'. Though his illustrator Leon Bennett represented Schultz as a moustacheless Bismarck,[2] the character of that sinister personage more foreshadows that of the Nazi war-lords, his Stahlstadt is a predecessor of the modern totalitarian state, and his published works suggestive of *Mein Kampf*.

But though Verne detested Prussian militarism he had no quarrel with the German people; he was too well informed and too objective not to realize and admire their fine qualities. To adapt the words he puts in the mouth of Dr Sarrasin, whose aim is not to retaliate on Stahlstadt but to bring it into friendly co-operation with Frankville:

> 'Why do they not use their rare intellectual gifts for the benefit of their fellow-creatures?'

[1] Patrick Moore, *Science and Fiction*.

[2] Edmondo Marcucci, *Les Illustrations des 'Voyages Étrangères' de Jules Verne*.

XI
Boxing the Compass

TO ADAPT a phrase coined by H. G. Wells, Verne's home was now a 'literary factory' in mass production. In addition to a number of his *Strange Journeys*, he had compiled a great non-fictional work, a History of Exploration. It involved deep research and is so comprehensive that it has been compared to a world history, and it effectively refuted the carpers who declared that Verne's knowledge of geography was only superficial.

The Discovery of the Earth appeared between 1878 and 1880 in three large copiously-illustrated volumes: *The Earliest Explorers*, beginning with Hanno of Carthage; *The Great Navigators of the Eighteenth Century*; *The Great Travellers of the Nineteenth Century*, ending about 1840. Now, of course, superseded by later research, it is described as 'rather dry and overcrammed with facts' (*assez aride et touffu*).[1] It livens up, however, when dealing with Verne's favourite characters, notably Marco Polo, Columbus[2] and, especially, Captain Cook.

Having finished this exacting task, and relieved his mind by his onslaught on Prussian militarism, Verne could work in lighter vein. His next book, *The Tribulations of a Chinese Gentleman* (1879), is one of his few comedies, though with a macabre touch suggestive of Poe.

Its hero, Kin-fo, is westernized and by contemporary standards modern. Wealthy and carefree, he should be perfectly happy, but he is bored and can enjoy nothing, not even the prospect of his marriage to a charming young widow to whom he is deeply attached. Tidings that he is ruined give him a chance of experiencing some emotion.

Having insured his life in the widow's favour, he instructs his best friend, the elderly philosopher Wang, to kill him, without warning, some time before the policy expires. To be in imminent expectation of death should certainly add excitement to life.

[1] René Escaich.

[2] The section on Columbus was republished separately.

It does, and more than he bargains for. Fresh tidings come that he is not ruined at all, and Wang has not only disappeared—finding himself unable to strike down his friend personally, he has confided the task to a robber chief who has no such scruples. . . .

Even in this book there is a characteristic touch of technical detail. Kin-fo, with his servant and two American detectives hired to protect him, are attacked by pirates and have to take to the water. They wear 'Boyton suits', inflatable garments which will keep them afloat and are equipped with paddles and a small mast and sail, to say nothing of food and drink, and a tiny chemical stove. They are proof against anything except a shark, and Verne may be relied on to supply even that.

The aftermath of the Indian Mutiny suggested his next book, *The Steam House* (1880). One of its ringleaders, the historic character Nana Sahib, had been implicated at a frightful massacre at Cawnpore, and his actual fate is unknown; Verne imagines him as having survived and as plotting another insurrection.

In the book his great enemy is Colonel Munro, whose wife had disappeared during the massacre; heart-broken by his bereavement, his one aim is vengeance. In the hope of distracting him from his grief, his friends plan a novel tour across India.

Banks, a skilled engineer, has constructed for a wealthy rajah a luxury caravan, consisting of two wheeled bungalows hauled by a steam elephant. (This, Mlle de la Fuÿe fancifully suggests, was 'an act of financial piety' to the real elephant which had stolen the limelight in the stage version of *Around the World*!) As after the rajah's death his heirs had been scared of the monster, Banks purchases Behemoth, as he called it, on the Colonel's behalf.

The journey is unexpectedly diversified. Proof against the attacks of wild beasts, the caravan enables the travellers to get some good shooting, but when it comes to running the gauntlet of a forest-fire that is another matter. Among other incidents, some fanatics, taking the caravan to be a Car of Juggernaut, try to immolate themselves under its wheels; and an unfriendly rajah challenges Behemoth to pit his strength against three magnificent elephants in flesh and blood.

These events are interspersed with the machinations of Nana Sahib, while flitting through the narrative goes a mysterious white woman, called the Roving Flame because she always carries a lighted torch, and regarded with veneration because she is obviously insane.

At last the Colonel falls into Nana Sahib's power. Bound helplessly across the mouth of a cannon, he is impassively waiting the moment of firing at dawn. Then the Roving Flame, still carrying her burning torch, flits perilously near the touch-hole. . . .

From the east Verne's mind now turned westwards. *The Giant Raft* (1881) is large enough to carry a whole village, including a church, down that giant river, the Amazon. Near its banks the heroes had come across the apparently endless tendril of a forest creeper; it is so long that their curiosity is aroused, and they decide to follow it to what proves to be a real 'surprise ending'.

The cipher which gives its name to the book's second part, *The Cryptogram*, is far more difficult than the elementary examples expounded by Poe, and Verne thought it insoluble. 'What analytical power! I'm literally confounded!' he exclaimed when he learned that it had been deciphered by a student of l'Ecole Polytechnique; having visited l'Ecole to see how this was done, he said that if he had known such a thing were possible he would have made the cipher more difficult still.[1]

The cryptogram is quite difficult enough, however, to baffle the character in the story, and it has to be deciphered at short notice. Failing this, an innocent man will be condemned to death.

In *The School for Robinsons* (1882), which would better have been entitled *The School for Crusoes* (it first appeared in England as *Godfrey Morgan: A Californian Mystery*), Verne satirized the whole 'desert island' type of literature. Here, though the uninhabited island is real, conditions upon it are synthetic: its owner, an American millionaire, had purchased it with the sole object of curing his young nephew of his romantic dreams of adventure.

After a sham shipwreck he lands the boy, together with an absurd professor of dancing and deportment, upon the island, and later provides him with a Man Friday, a negro who has to be 'rescued' from apparently cannibalistic savages. He menaces him with wild beasts, but they are stuffed and actuated by springs. Then perils appear which, far from being synthetic, are only too real. . . . The story is written in a silly facetious style worthy of its subject.

While writing these books, Verne was seeking much-needed rest

[1] Maurice d'Ocagne, 'Jules Verne raconté par le fils de l'un de ses amis', in *Hommes et Choses de Science*.

and relaxation, and escaping from the lion-hunters, by cruising with congenial friends in the *St Michel III*. His first trip, in 1878, was made from Nantes round Spain and into the Mediterranean. He was much amused to hear one of his guests, a firm believer in the possibilities of an international language, apostrophizing the Pillars of Hercules in a forerunner of Esperanto, Volapük.

He did not completely escape lionizing, however. Banquets and other entertainments, including a boar-hunt, were arranged in his honour, and he occasionally invited local personalities to dine on his yacht. Had he wished, he could have hob-nobbed with the great.

Having no wish for such company, he was not too polite about showing it. When after his return he and Honorine were invited to some important function, he did not trouble either to reply or to tell her—to her great annoyance when she found out too late. When, hearing that he was off the Isle of Wight during the Cowes Regatta, the Royal Yacht Squadron invited him to attend a reception given by the Prince of Wales, again he did not trouble to reply. Murmuring something to the effect that a man could get no peace anywhere, he simply sailed away.

His next cruise, in 1879, took him on another journey to Scotland and Norway, and included a visit to Ireland. It may have led him to write his second Scottish story, *The Green Ray* (1882): some of its characters are derived from Dickens and Scott, but one was a child of his own fertile brain.

In its opening chapter appear two benevolent uncles, avowedly based on 'the most worthy characters that had ever emanated from the imagination of Dickens', the Brothers Cheeryble of *Nicholas Nickelby*. Their niece is charming but wayward, resembling 'that adorable heroine of *Rob Roy*, Diana Vernon'. When they tactfully suggest a husband, she flabbergasts them by refusing to marry until she has seen the Green Ray.

This Ray, which Verne describes in flowery terms, is occasionally seen flashing upwards from the setting sun just as the last vestige of its rim vanishes below a clear sea-horizon. One of the legends it has evoked asserts that nobody who has witnessed this 'living light' can ever err in matters affecting the heart.

Poetry apart, the girl acts wisely in finding an excuse for putting off her marriage to the suitor whom her uncles favour, an anti-hero and a highbrow at once. If Mr Gradgrind, of *Hard Times*, had had a scientifically minded nephew, he might well resemble the prospective bridegroom, endowed with the preposterous name of Aristobulus Ursiclos.[1] To him the sea is no source of mystery and awe, but a mere solution of sodium chloride, and by analysing human tears he has shown that their sole function is to lubricate the eyeball.

Fortunately the girl has another suitor, who co-operates with the uncles in trying to enable her to see the famous Green Ray, and the bulk of the story is devoted to keeping it out of sight until the last chapter.

The story includes a heroic rescue in Fingal's Cave, and this gives Verne an opportunity of describing its unique geological structure. Its general tone is however poetic, its author letting himself go as he revels in the scenic wonders and romantic associations of Scotland.

Paul Verne wrote an account[2] of his brother's third cruise, when in 1881 the two travelled through the North Sea and along the Eider into the Kiel roadstead. Though in Germany, as elsewhere, Jules Verne was cordially welcomed, even he could not be allowed to see anything of the country's armaments industry. However, he saw enough to realize that his account, in *The Begum's Fortune*, of its potentialities had not been exaggerated, and he looked with well-justified forebodings at its future effects upon the world's peace.

From the north he now turned south, both physically and in thought. His fourth cruise, in 1884, took him again into the Mediterranean, seeking background for a story he had in mind. Again he was lionized, but for a time he was in a more tractable mood and did not scurry angrily away. When the 'Lobsters' of Gibraltar carried him off in triumph to their mess they so filled him with punch that, as he said later, 'he could no longer stand upright on his Pillars of Hercules'!

At Oran, the cruise became a family party, for Verne's wife and son joined him. Soon, however, it had to be interrupted, for the sea became so rough that Honorine insisted on travelling to Tunis by land. This led them into experiences ranging from an appalling meal in a verminous inn to the oriental luxury of the Bey's private railway

[1] Apparently meaning 'best in counsel' and 'a little bear'.

[2] Published with the French edition of *The Giant Raft*, but not translated into English, and hardly likely to be, as it is not of great interest; its author seems to have had some obscure quarrel, perhaps on technical grounds, with the English pilot.

train. When another spell of bad weather forced them to land on some bare sand-dunes, Verne delightedly pretended that he was shipwrecked and performed a fierce war-dance round an imaginary camp-fire. Finally, after the vessel had really been in danger of shipwreck during a violent gale, Honorine lost her taste for sea-travel, and on reaching Italy she insisted on their returning home overland.

This kept Verne from collecting all the local colour he had hoped for, but he had certainly gained much, including a first-hand experience of imminent peril at sea. He had seen the ruins of Carthage and the antiquities of Malta, and he had insisted on a visit to Mount Etna, for he had never lost his interest in volcanoes. And could he pass through Milan without studying the works of Leonardo da Vinci, who had foretold the flying machine? Verne had long had a great admiration for that artist, and had once written a verse comedy about him and his platonic love for the lady whom he had immortalized as the Mona Lisa.

Verne's hopes of travelling through Italy incognito were frustrated and he had to put up with more lionizing. It bored him as much as ever: when the Venetians, after greeting him with a firework display and other illuminations, sent a laurel crown into his bedroom he first pretended to be asleep and then hung it casually on an urn.

Though normally he shunned contact with the great, there was one with whom he felt it a privilege to be accorded an interview. This was Pope Leo XIII, who praised not so much the scientific value of his works as their moral high and spiritual value. So deeply moved by his encouragement and blessing was Verne that he left the audience in tears.

The book for which he had sought local colour in the Mediterranean, *Matthias Sandorf*, will be discussed later, along with another, *The Archipelago on Fire*, which resulted from the cruise. A third, *Keraban the Pig-headed* (1883), had a short-lived career as a play and makes a mediocre book.

Its hero is a Turk so determined not to pay a tax for crossing the Bosphorus by boat that when he has to visit Scutari on the opposite shore he insists on travelling by land—round the Black Sea! On arriving after varied mishaps, he finds he must return to Constantinople at once, but he still refuses to pay the tax. Without recourse to a flying-machine or other science fictional expedient,

Verne gets him across in a possible, though unlikely, surprise ending. . . .

Verne even sent his imagination as far afield as South Africa. The scene of *The Southern Star Mystery* (1884) is Griqualand, Cape Colony; the diamond-workings are vividly described and the evil effects of the greed for wealth are emphasized.

The hero, a young French scientist, is in love with the charming daughter of a brutal dissipated Englishman; for her sake he gives up pure research to join in the hunt for diamonds, but at the same time he tries to make the gems synthetically by exposing the blue clay in which they are found to intense pressure and heat. Imagine his joy when he finds in the ruins of his furnace a diamond of immense size and incalculable value!

But it brings him nothing but trouble, including a threat to his life from the irate diamond-diggers, who realize that his process would knock the bottom out of the market. Suddenly the gem vanishes, and the hero's native servant, known to be light-fingered, is in danger of being lynched as a thief. When he runs away the hero, convinced of his innocence, follows him, meeting with unprecedented perils in the jungle.

There are a number of surprise twists to the narrative; one concerns a virtuous Boer who explains how his people had been driven from pillar to post, and he himself defrauded, by the land-grabbing English. His own personal enemy is the brutal dissipated Englishman, whom some French critics regarded as a caricature of Cecil Rhodes!

In 1885 Verne gave another fancy-dress ball, not on so vast a scale as that earlier one, but still quite ambitious. His house was placarded as 'The Great Inn of the World Tour', and he and Honorine, suitably clad, figured as the innkeeper and his wife presiding over an immense pot of stew—not, of course, the only food to be served during the evening! It is significant that Verne seemed able to relax in company and enjoy himself only when at sea or in disguise.

Greatly as he had enjoyed his cruise in the Mediterranean, and brilliantly as he had written about that region and about South Africa, he was still, as he told one of his illustrators, longing to see a northern sky once more after this dazzling southern light. Unable to do so in fact, he did so in his imagination, using the local colour he had gained on his earlier visits to Norway.

The theme of *The Lottery Ticket* (1886) is a variant of the Poe-esque 'message found in a bottle'. Its Norwegian heroine bids a tearful farewell to her intended, a fisherman who sets out for the waters off Newfoundland dropping vague hints that their fortune will be made when he returns.

He does not return, however, and nothing more is heard of him until a bottle is found saying that his boat has been wrecked and enclosing the lottery ticket he had purchased. The girl, to whom he bequeaths it, realizes that this must be the fortune he had been hinting at.

The episode is widely publicized, and because of its strange history the ticket is thought to be 'lucky' and bound to win the first prize. Tempting as are the offers she received, she refuses, because of its sentimental value, to part with it. Finally, however, as in an old-fashioned melodrama, she is forced to do so, to redeem the mortgage on the family home. . . .

For the only time in his life Verne wrote a book in collaboration, his associate being so extraordinary a person he might have figured in one of the *Strange Journeys*. Born in Corsica in 1845, Paschal Grousset plunged violently into political journalism, became a leader in the Commune, and was banished to the penal settlements of New Caledonia. Having escaped, he at last returned to France under an amnesty, and was several times elected to the Chamber of Deputies as a 'radical socialist'.

He wrote under two pseudonyms as well as his own name, on a wide variety of subjects. *Conquest of the Moon*, by that 'voluminous jack of all trades André Laurie', has been aptly described as 'quite the most preposterous journey to another world of the century'.[1]

What shares he, and what Verne, had in their combined effort is uncertain. My own surmise is that 'Laurie' was responsible for the melodramatic plot and Verne for the background, placed among the Arctic solitudes that he loved and inspired by a feat of exploration that must have aroused his enthusiasm.

Attempts to find the North-west Passage having been given up as hopeless, in 1878 the Swedish explorer Nordenskiold had set out to find the North-east Passage, round the North Cape and the Siberian coast. Held up by bad weather, he had to winter not far from the Bering Strait, not completing his journey until the following spring.

[1] Roger Lancelyn Green, *Into Other Worlds*.

Had Verne been helping to write *Salvage from the Cynthia* (1885) in English he might, with his addiction to puns, have called it *The Boy on the Buoy*, for the salvage consists of a life-buoy to which is lashed a cradle. Its occupant, a young baby whose clothing indicates wealthy parents, is adopted and named Erik by the fisherman who rescued him, and his outstanding intelligence enables him to become a ship's master. The plot of the story turns on his efforts, thwarted by an unscrupulous enemy, to discover his own identity.

For the purposes of the story, Nordenskild reports finding on the Siberian coast a seaman who has a clue to the secret, but only Verne could have thought of the route by which the young hero tries to find him, through the North-west Passage. In actual fact this had baffled everyone who had attempted it, but Erik simply crashes his way through it.

His encounter with the villain involves scenes of battle amid the ice-floes reminiscent of one of Kipling's poems. Continuing westward along the North-east Passage, Erik accomplishes a feat which, according to the Royal Geographical Society, no real-life explorer has so much as attempted: he has circumnavigated the North Pole!

After such a feat, the disclosure of Erik's identity comes rather as an anticlimax. Distressed at not even knowing what country he belonged to, he felt there was one which he would above all prefer, because of 'her splendid traditions, her stirring history, the harvest of ideals which she had sown throughout the world'. And what country was that? Knowing the nationality of the two authors, need the reader ask?

XII
Triumph and Disaster

FOR SEVERAL years Verne had neglected the art-form he had founded. In 1886 he returned to it with—literally, as the story shows—a great flourish of trumpets. Serialized in the *Journal des Débats*, his new story described one of the strangest of his *Strange Journeys* carried out in a manner that makes it, in spite of the narrative's manifest imperfections, another triumph of science fiction.

The Clipper of the Clouds, as its English translation is called—its original title was *Robur le Conquérant*—is, it cannot be denied, one of those disappointments, a brilliant idea badly worked out; my impression is that it was written against time, as though Verne were meeting his editor's demands for copy. The invention is described in graphic detail, as are two spectacular rescues and a hazardous crossing of Antarctica, and the climax is magnificent. Delighted with these, editor and publisher may have been pressing for early delivery of the MS and Verne may have been making up his story as he went along.

It opens with an absurd duel, irrelevant except that it introduces inexplicable aerial phenomena which in modern times would be attributed to a 'Flying Saucer'. A trumpet sounds, and mysterious lights gleam, high in the air; the world's savants offer conflicting opinions, but all agree in ridiculing a Chinese astronomer, who suggests a 'flying machine'—until earth's loftiest buildings are incredibly adorned with flags displaying an emblem never before seen.

Thereafter Verne, for want of further inspiration, seems to have been trying, not over-successfully, to recapture the magic of his earlier successes. The members of the Gun Club of Baltimore had been quaint and almost lovable; those of the Weldon Institute of Philadelphia are mannerless boors. Determined to construct an 'aerostat' (dirigible balloon), they are shouting one another down and are on the verge of violence over a trifling technical detail, whether its screw propeller should be at the prow or the stern, when——

A newcomer, even more uncouth and boorish than themselves, announces that he is called Robur and that he is worthy of that name—derived, either direct or through that of the explosive Roburite, from the Latin for 'strength'. He derides as impracticable their idea of an aerostat, insisting that the conquest of the air can be accomplished only by an 'aeronef' (heavier-than-air flying machine). Mutual recriminations lead to an attempt to mob, or possibly to lynch, him, but he disappears unscathed with a crackle of revolver shots.

The leaders of the Club's two rival cliques are still disputing during their evening stroll when they are suddenly pounced on, bound, gagged, blindfolded, kidnapped, and deposited in what seems like a prison-cell.

The story now resembles an inferior version of *Twenty Thousand Leagues*, with an 'aeronef' instead of a submarine and the brutal mannerless Robur instead of the coldly courteous Captain Nemo. He at least had a plausible excuse for holding his three prisoners incommunicado, his desire to conceal his existence from the world.

For Robur there is no such excuse. He presumably wishes to convince his two captives of the aeronef's superiority over the aerostat, and for this all he need do is to take them for a brief flight, give a demonstration of his vessel's speed and soaring-power, and then return them, suitably chastened, to their homes.

Instead he imprisons them and their negro servant indefinitely, point-blank refuses to release them, and takes them for a flight of indeterminate length. As this includes a crossing of Africa, there is more than a suggestion here of the balloon *Victoria*. The flight ends surprisingly, and the end of the book, with its unexpected transformation of Robur's character, is more surprising still.

Whoever chose the title of the English version certainly had a flash of inspiration, for the story's real hero is not Robur himself but his invention, well described in the memorably alliterative phrase 'The Clipper of the Clouds', for that is exactly what it looks like.

The failure of Nadar's *Géant* had destroyed Verne's faith in dirigible balloons, and he now felt that the aircraft of the future would be the helicopter. The notes made by Leonardo da Vinci, which he had had an opportunity of studying in Italy, had foreshadowed this, and he knew that in 1875 a steam-driven helicopter had made a flight of twenty seconds' duration, reaching a height of about fourteen yards. Trivial hop though this might appear, Verne realized its significance for the future.

The *Albatross*, the aeronef which dominates Verne's story, is a helicopter resembling a clipper-ship, her hull, or airframe, having a flat deck above which are three deckhouses and the steersman's cabin. Instead of masts and sails, she has thirty-seven slim uprights, each carrying two contra-rotating screws, and she is propelled by contra-rotating screws at prow and stern. Her motive power is of course electricity, and—again of course—it is 'not everybody's electricity', but is generated by batteries of unprecedented strength invented by Robur himself.

Dr R. C. Pankhurst, of the Aerodynamics Department of the National Physical Laboratory, comments that although this array of seventy-four lifting screws would be far less efficient than one larger screw, the *Albatross* foreshadows certain developments of modern helicopteral practice. One might add that the material of which she is built, compressed paper, foreshadows the modern development of plastics. Both in the illustrations to the book's original edition, and in the model displayed in the little-known Jules Verne Museum in the Palais de Paris, the *Clipper of the Clouds* is impressive and picturesque, and she served as the prototype of the flying-machines in later imaginative stories until these were superseded, even before their invention, by the modern airplane.

So in 1886 Verne seemed at the zenith of his career. For years he had enjoyed a long succession of triumphs, from the enthusiastic public welcome of *Five Weeks in a Balloon* onwards, and culminating in the audience given him by the Pope.

His books, translated into many tongues, were being read almost all round the world, and two had been successfully dramatized; though naturally they varied in quality, almost all were good and some were a valuable addition to the world's literature. The art-form he had founded was developing wonderfully in his own and other hands. And now *The Clipper of the Clouds* was adding to his reputation.

He had enjoyed a number of delightful cruises in his much-loved *St Michel III*, and he was looking forward to others. He may have planned to visit Madeira and the other Atlantic islands, like the heroes of one of his posthumous works, or to visit Iceland, like those of one of his earliest. He may even have dreamed of a cruise round the world. These hopes were never to be fulfilled.

In March 1886, he was returning home when a youth dashed towards him and opened fire with a revolver. Though hit in the leg, Verne staggered up to his assailant and disarmed him. Then he collapsed. In spite of a long course of treatment, involving several painful operations, he was crippled for life.

For a time this episode was well publicized and then suddenly the press were silent about it, as though they had come across a scandal and were sympathetically trying to hush it up. So indeed they were, for its victim was amazed to find, when he recognized his assailant, that this was his own nephew, Gaston Verne![1]

Suffering from a nervous breakdown brought on by overwork and developing into persecution mania, the youth had escaped from supervision and been wandering about Amiens. Whether he recognized his uncle, and if so why he attacked him, is unknown; the uncharitable suggestion has been made[2] that Jules Verne's sincere interest in his nephew's welfare had made him behave—to use an almost Vernian pun—too much like a Dutch uncle, and that this had aroused a smouldering resentment which at last expressed itself in a revolver-shot.

During his long convalescence Jules Verne was assailed by two bereavements, the death of his mother and that of his publisher, Hetzel. He felt both keenly, for he had been deeply attached to his mother, and Hetzel had become almost a father-figure.[3] True, Verne was on the most friendly terms with the latter's son, also called Jules Hetzel, who had taken over the family business, but this was not the same. Moreover, for once the time-honoured joke had been literally true: the old man had been not so much a publisher as a friend.

Unable to work systematically, Verne sought respite, during the long hours of pain and sleeplessness, in composing innumerable cryptograms and acrostics. If crosswords—here the unavoidable pun is unintentional—had then been in vogue, how warmly he would have welcomed them!

[1] The attempt to hush it up was still being continued as late as 1928, for Mme Allotte de la Fuÿe, when she describes the episode in her biography of Verne, does not divulge the culprit's name!

[2] M. Moré, *Le Très Curieux Jules Verne*.

[3] M. Moré, *ib.*

'The Steam House', from *Tigers and Traitors*

Aeronef *versus* Aerostat, from *Clipper in the Clouds*

Jules Verne in October 1902

'Onward to immortality and eternal youth'; Jules Verne's tomb at Amiens

At last able to limp about, he went to Nantes to help settle affairs under his mother's will. Then he embarked for a cruise on the *St Michel III*.

So long as she was in the sheltered waters of the Loire he managed to keep his feet. But when she crossed the bar and began to feel the waves he silently went below and the yacht returned to port. As soon as he could find a purchaser she was sold.

Verne had prided himself on his sea-legs. Now he, who had been not merely her owner but virtually one of the ship's company, could not bear to spend his time no longer on the bridge beside the captain or at the wheel, but reclining in a deck-chair like a mere passenger and having to go below at the slightest sign of bad weather.

Neither could he endure life at Nantes, the scene of his boyish dreams and of his venture upon the *Coralie*, where he would be in sight and hearing of the ships on the river. Nor could he return to Paris, the scene of his adolescent dreams and his first success.

Determinedly turning his back upon the sea, he settled down in his home in Amiens, where his friends and family lived, where he had many connections and where he had his study and his works of reference. Above his house was a tower[1] which gave a splendid view across the city: no longer could he mount the ladder to this as though going up to the bridge or the crow's-nest, but below it were rooms more easily accessible in which he could work.

Realizing that he would be a landsman for the rest of his life, he began on his next book.

[1] Similar to that described so enthusiastically in *The Secret of Wilhelm Storitz*.

XIII
Town-planning in Fact and Fiction

NOBODY who knew Verne was surprised that in spite of his disability he kept on with his work. What did startle his family and friends was his decision to stand, in 1883, for election to the Municipal Council of Amiens. What was more, he scandalized many of them, and reduced his wife to tears, by standing on the 'Left' side.

Even his new allies were doubtful, suspicious of what they called 'M. Verne's historical liberalism'. On the other hand, they realized the prestige of his name; and if he, as a well-meaning but inexperienced amateur, were to be too officious, no doubt these hardened politicians would find some way of keeping him in order.

Verne himself could not see what all the fuss was about; his avowed aim was solely to make himself useful and to bring about certain urban reforms: he had almost openly chosen the Left side merely because that gave him the best chance of being elected, and certainly he was the last man to 'toe the party line'. Why, he asked, must people mix politics and Christianity with administrative questions? He himself was all for Order, and he wanted to develop a balanced reasonable party with a respect for justice and culture and lofty ideals. Meanwhile, he added rather cynically,[1] the vagaries of the extremists would give him much-needed entertainment. Moreover, though he did not say so, all was local colour that came to his net.

Elected after a somewhat acrimonious campaign, he took his duties very seriously, and he was especially interested in the Council's cultural activities and social services. He devoted much attention to the municipal theatre, and—for he had always delighted in the circus—he tried to improve the conditions of the wandering entertainers, the troupes of acrobats and so forth, who visited Amiens.

This gave him literary material which he later used with effect. The heroine of *Carpathian Castle* (1892) is an opera singer who comes to a tragic end while on the stage, and in *Foundling Mick* (1893) is a graphic account of a theatrical performance which goes wrong.

[1] In a letter, quoted by Allott, to a 'dear donkey' of a friend.

To the adventures of a wandering circus he devoted a whole book. These adventures are far from conventional: *César Cascabel* (1890) is not what Allott's description, 'the hard-luck story of a family of entertainers', would lead the reader to expect.

César himself is a professional strong man and his wife his female counterpart; their two sons are acrobats and their little daughter a tight-rope walker; in their troupe are a grotesque clown, two performing dogs, a voluble parrot, and a monkey. After a successful trip across the United States to the Far West, they are about to return home to France when all their money is stolen.

Undeterred by their inability to pay the fare, they decide to make the journey overland through Alaska and Siberia, floating their caravan across the Bering Straits on the pack-ice! The Russian nobleman who accompanies them proves to be a political exile 'wanted by the police', and two ruffianly sailors whom they have befriended mean to betray him for the sake of the reward.

During their journey the Cascabels enter into a friendly contest with some Red Indians, whose braves outmatch them in juggling, 'forming pyramids', and tight-rope walking. Is there nothing in their répertoire to make civilized showmanship superior to traditional native skill? Later they are imprisoned and threatened with slavery; cannot they turn their varied talents to good effect? . . .

Verne's success on the Municipal Council evoked the suggestion that he should go in seriously for national politics; with his prestige he might even aspire to the Presidency of France. He rejected such notions with scorn: other considerations apart, this would interfere with his literary work.

Though municipal service was a new venture for him, he had long had a keen interest in town-planning. This he had shown years earlier, in a paper he had read in 1875 to the Amiens Academy of Arts, Letters and Sciences. Though *Amiens in the Year 2000* A.D. contains local allusions which no doubt delighted his audience but are cryptic to the modern reader, it has a more general interest.[1]

Some of his forecasts are ironical, not to say sarcastic. The ladies' dresses have trains so long they have to be borne on 'tiny metal wheels which murmur pleasantly over the sandy paths'; their hats resemble a Brazilian jungle with 'tangled lianas, arborescent plants, tropical birds, jaguars and snakes'; their hair-dos are 'so embar-

[1] It is included in the volume *Yesterday and Tomorrow*.

rassingly large and heavy they have to be supported on a little wicker cage'.

Even in his sarcasm Verne displays a certain prescience. Music is transmitted over the telegraph wires, so that when a 'famous ivory pounder' strikes a key in Paris, the same note resounds from the piano-strings in places as far apart as London and Pekin. The music of the future does not seem human, 'nor for that matter, celestial either'! There is 'nothing musical in these phrases, no melody, no time, no harmony. The quintessence of Wagner? The triumph of discord. An effect like that of orchestral instruments being tuned before the curtain rises.' The title of the piece is 'Reverie in a minor key on the square of the hypotenuse'—and perhaps neither this title nor that type of music would be out of place in certain modern performances.

In this Amiens of the future sickness has been banished by the simple plan of paying the doctor so long as the patient keeps well; he diagnoses by taking a graph of the pulse-beats, but when asked what is amiss he simply replies 'Um! Um' ('Yes, I know that answer', comments Verne.) Marriage has been encouraged by the even more simple plan of a ruinous tax on bachelors, with the result that children swarm in such numbers that the babies have to be fed by machinery.

Education is purely scientific, commercial and industrial; the last of the classical scholars made such frightful howlers that the study of Latin was suppressed.

Mechanical developments are astounding: one American machine turns a fleece into a complete suit of clothes; another converts a live pig into two hams, one York and one Westphalian; and another transforms a calf into a pair of newly polished shoes and a steaming blanquette of veal. Then a Regional Competition shows that

> 'Everything had altered in this world; everything had followed the line of progress! Ideas, customs, industry, commerce, agriculture, all had been transformed. Only the words of the Ministerial Delegate's speech were what they had always been:
>
> '"Gentlemen, it is with renewed pleasure that I find myself once more . . ."'

But, here, Verne said, he woke up.

The Begum's Fortune (1879) includes two contrasted types of town-planning. Herr Schultz's Stahlstadt is a totalitarian Utopia, with everything, including a Gestapo, that the most exacting Nazi could desire. Its workmen are under military discipline, bound by oath never to reveal any of its secrets, their correspondence censored and limited to their own family; anyone who enquires too closely into its mysteries is quickly—though, to give Herr Schultz his due, painlessly—eliminated.

Its counterpart, Frankville, in spite of its boasted freedom, has the restrictions that a fanatic for hygiene might be expected to impose. All its citizens must earn their living, and idlers are excluded. While leaving scope for individual tastes, houses have to conform to certain general rules; carpets and wall-papers, as possible 'nests of infection', are forbidden, as are eiderdown quilts and heavy coverlets. All washing is disinfected in the public laundry before being returned to its owner, and even the toddlers of four 'are accustomed to such strict cleanliness that they consider a spot on their simple clothes as quite a disgrace'.

Ordinary easy-going people might find either city rather a strain to live in. Both, however, have their redeeming features. Most of the workers in Stahlstadt are 'quiet and gentle', and they have a library and a 'very tolerable band'. Here a pit-boy has some bats and a tame rat to play with and a friendly horse to fondle, whereas it is hard to imagine the children of Frankville, or their parents for that matter, being allowed anything so unhygienic as a pet. Nevertheless, in spite of its founder's fanaticism, much in this latter city displays admirable conceptions of town-planning, and shows that, here as elsewhere, Verne's ideas were in advance of his age.

In 1885 Gordon Bennett, editor of the *New York Herald*, asked Verne to write an imaginative account of life in the United States in a thousand years' time.[1] He must however have been disappointed with the result, for it did not appear until 1889 and then not in the *Herald* but in another American periodical, the *Forum*.

Rather surprisingly, considering its interest, this forecast was printed during Verne's lifetime only in the *Mémoires* of the Amiens Academy; it was not published in France until it was included in the posthumous collection *Yesterday and Tomorrow*. Several altera-

[1] Andreev, *Préface aux Oeuvres Complètes en U.R.S.S.* Translated in *Europe*, April/May 1955.

tions were made in the French version, including the insertion of a mildly improper incident which, Verne may have thought, contemporary transatlantic readers might regard as 'shocking'.[1]

This discrepancy led the French critic Etienne Cluzel to go further into the matter, and he was amazed to find that a number of the ideas Verne had used seemed to have been taken from another forecast, *Le Vingtième Siècle,* by the French science-fiction writer Marcel Robida. They included what Robida called the 'telephonoscope' and Verne called the 'phototelephone', transmitting both sound and vision by wire from caller to receiver; the *'théâtre chez soi'*, which in Robida's illustration looks amazingly like a modern television set; the 'aeronef-omnibus'; electro-pneumatic tube trains; the delivery of food by tube from factory to home; and the telephone newspaper with its serial.[2]

Verne makes no acknowledgment of his debt to Robida; but as the latter's ideas of the submarine of the future were obviously derived from the *Nautilus,* he may have thought that this was fair give and take; the two authors may indeed have come to an amicable arrangement to exchange ideas. Probably, however, it was because he did not want to be unfair to his confrère that Verne did not publish his own forecast in France.

In the Twenty-ninth Century : The Day of an American Journalist in 2889 describes a mechanized world largely run by electricity: once again this is 'not everybody's electricity' but it is generated either by sunshine or by the earth's internal heat; it has transformed agriculture and, by making aerial navigation possible, has revolutionized commerce. The telephone, as already mentioned, now also transmits vision, and a transatlantic tube links Paris with Centropolis, the new capital of the United States—and virtually of the whole world.

It is here that Francis Bennett, the suppositious descendant and successor of Gordon Bennett, and editor of the *Earth Herald,* reigns as mankind's uncrowned king. At one moment he is an editor directing his contributors and technical staff; at another he is a potentate with ambassadors seeking his aid.

'You've got to dissect,' he tells an author. 'It isn't with a pen one

[1] Étienne Cluzel, 'Un Livre Negligé ou les Incroyables Anticipations de Jules Verne'. Included in the *Bulletin du Bibliophile et de Bibliothécaire,* 1959.

[2] Étienne Cluzel, 'Les Anticipations de Jules Verne et celles de Marcel Robida', *ib.* 1961.

writes nowadays, it's with a scalpel.' He berates his scientists for failing to get in touch with Jupiter, as they have done with the inner planets, and instructs them to turn the moon round to ascertain if its far side is inhabited. He is annoyed when a fine day precludes his advertisements from being projected on to the clouds: 'We really can't be at the mercy of the fine weather!' he rebukes his meteorological experts.

It is he who decides which lines of research are to be pursued and which discontinued. An investigation into atomic structure; a scheme for transporting whole cities in bulk, with startling effects on land values; a proposal to melt the polar ice—these are given various degrees of encouragement. But the cynical journalist has no patience for the visionary who hopes to find a cure for the common cold.

Bennett settles the most pressing political problem, the proliferation of the Chinese, by a death penalty on anyone who contravenes the birth-control laws. 'A child too many? . . . A father less! That will keep things balanced.'

France is, in theory, independent, ruling all Western Europe; but, reading between the lines, she is obviously an American satellite state. Certainly there is no doubt as to the status of Britain, as Bennett makes clear to the English Ambassador.

> '"But England is only one of our colonies, one of our finest. Don't count on our ever consenting to give her up."
>
> '"So that's the end," the Consul was overwhelmed. "The United Kingdom, Canada, and New Britain belong to the Americans, India to the Russians, and Australia and New Zealand to themselves! Of all that once was England, what is left? . . . Nothing!"
>
> '"Nothing, sir?" retorted Francis Bennett. "Nothing? Well, what about Gibraltar?"'

The whole forecast, like Verne's 'dream' of Amiens a hundred years hence, showed that he did not regard the future with unmixed enthusiasm and that he was looking with disquiet at the growing Americanization of Europe.

His interest in town-planning appears in several of his other stories; the cities built by the heroes of *Mathias Sandorf* and *The Survivors of the 'Jonathan'* are attractively and efficiently laid out.

During his municipal service Verne learned much about the realities of politics and the extremes to which its votaries are led.

This theme appears in the only story he wrote expressly for juvenile readers, *Two Years' Holiday* (1888).

Some schoolboys from New Zealand are embarked for a cruise in the Pacific when their vessel is mysteriously set adrift, their only companion being the Negro cabin-boy. When she is wrecked on a desert island, the castaways have to fend for themselves, as they do very efficiently on true Robinson Crusoe lines. Then, having ensured their safety and comfort, they organize classes and continue their education!

Though most are New Zealanders, one of the most leaderly is an American. Another, Briant, is French, and is said to be based on a boy whom Verne knew and who later became Premier of France, Aristide Briand.[1] Resentful at being ruled by 'foreigners', one of the older New Zealanders aspires to leadership, and after an acrimonious electoral campaign, these 'schoolboy politics', as Kenneth Allott calls them, culminate in the withdrawal of the malcontent and his followers to form their own colony. And this at a time when unity is essential, for the boys are one and all threatened by the landing of some vicious pirates! The ingenious method they devise to locate their enemies without revealing their own presence is typical. . . .

The results of Verne's political experience are most drastically shown in his satire *Propeller Island* (1895). This, too, displays his love of music and it embodies his childish dreams of the Ile Feydeau's drifting out to sea. Among its heroes are the members of a talented string quartet; infuriated at being kidnapped, they are reconciled on finding that they are to be the honoured and well-remunerated guests of a community of American millionaires dwelling, literally, on a synthetic island.

Standard Island, as it is called, resembles in construction the 'Mulberry Harbours' of the Second World War, but it is navigable and self-propelled; two immense generating stations operate screws on its port and starboard sides. For the possibility of steering the island by regulating their speed, its 'inventor' got much helpful advice from his brother Paul.

Its capital, Milliard City, gave Jules Verne his head for imaginative town-planning. The town is built in American style, with all its streets at right angles, but the actual design of the houses is left to the ideas of their architects or the whims of their wealthy clients;

[1] M. Moré, *Le Très Curieux Jules Verne*.

their gardens resemble small parks, and the city squares are 'carpeted with lawns of quite an English freshness'. There is an ornate pseudo-Gothic cathedral and an austere Protestant church, for the only religions recognized on the island are Roman Catholicism and Calvinism.

Transport is accomplished partly by electric trams, partly by moving pavements; correspondence by telephone, teleprinter, or telautograph. The latter, a method of transmitting handwriting telegraphically, was a contemporary invention which promised well but never came into general use; in the story it serves for shopping, signing business documents, getting married or—'that's what keeps the wires busiest'—divorced.

The island itself is over four miles long and three wide; it draws thirty feet of water with a freeboard of twenty feet and it has its own lighthouse, harbours and defensive batteries. Most of its surface is covered with soil on which it grows its own crops, largely by electro-culture, and feeds its own livestock. It is lit by 'artificial moons' of 5000 candle-power and serviced electrically. Disappointingly, however, and unlike Captain Nemo and Robur, it uses the conventional 'everybody's electricity', generated neither by solar heat nor from the ocean, but by dynamos driven by oil-fuelled engines.

A regular service of steamers keeps Standard Island in touch with America, meeting it at assigned ports of call along its route as it carries its wealthy population for an unending luxury cruise across the Pacific in search of the most picturesque islands and the most favourable climate. Its course can be accurately charted, for it has its own observatory.

Yet—and here Verne's experience of political controversy came in—the island has one essential weakness, the mutual hostility between the romantic Catholics from the Southern States of the Union and the dour Calvinists from the North. An exiled monarch, said to be based on the abdicated Pedro II of Brazil, might have held the balance even, but he refuses to be drawn into politics. . . .

Relieved of its excessive geographical and ethnological detail, and of the atrocious puns perpetrated by one member of the quartet, the narrative is full of excitement and interest. A satire worthy of Voltaire or Swift or George Orwell, *Propeller Island* is none the less among the classics which science fiction owes to Jules Verne.

XIV
'In Freedom's Cause'

VERNE's love of freedom is implicit in all his narratives and explicit in some, *The Lottery Ticket* including a reference to the dislike of the Norwegians at being ruled by the King of Sweden, and *The Southern Star Mystery* containing one of his many protests against English imperialism. Its leading exponent is of course Captain Nemo, bitterly waging a one-man war against the British.

Two books whose theme is the struggle for freedom drew local colour and background from Verne's last cruise in the Mediterranean. *The Archipelago on Fire* (1884) centres on the revolt of the Greeks against Turkish rule that culminated in the Battle of Navarino—not so much with the revolt itself, however, as with its aftermath, the suppression of piracy in the Eastern Mediterranean. The pirates are led by a ferocious Greek renegade, and a privateer with a crew of mixed nationality, commanded by a French officer, is sent to capture or slay him. After varied adventures, the privateer finds herself hemmed in by a pirate flotilla; unable, even had she wished, to escape, she is outnumbered, outmanned and outgunned, but her commander and crew are determined to fight on to the last. . . .

Mathias Sandorf (1885), one of Verne's most ambitious works, is dedicated to the younger Dumas and to the memory of the elder Dumas, and its author had tried to make it 'the *Monte Cristo* of the *Strange Journeys*'. But it is only in general outline that it follows the earlier book: its hero, betrayed and thrown into prison, makes a dramatic escape and seeks revenge on the traitors.

Sandorf, whose imprisonment is due to his having attempted to organize a Hungarian revolt against Austrian rule, resembles not so much Dumas' hero as Captain Nemo, but a Nemo with some idea of social responsibility and a sense of humour. (And with enough common sense to ensure that the luxurious fittings of his vessel are fastened down securely—can someone, possibly his brother Paul, have been chaffing Verne about this?) Unlike Nemo, too, he is discriminating and seeks revenge not wholesale but solely on the guilty.

It must be confessed that, in spite of his wealth and other advantages, he makes rather heavy weather of it. Now known as Dr Antekirtt, he is a scientist and a physician, combining the lore of the East with the science of the West. He is moreover a hypnotist: here, as in the cipher of the 'grille' type with which the story opens, the influence of Poe is obvious. His followers are devoted to him, especially two delightful acrobats whom he has befriended: the Herculean strength of the one is as serviceable as the agility and quick wits of the other.

Though rather on the long side—the attempt to dramatize it was unsuccessful—*Mathias Sandorf* is one of its author's successes and verges on science fiction. Dr Antekirtt, who owns an island off Tripoli, converts it into a small-scale private Gibraltar, and defends it against the pirates by a flotilla including vessels which resemble submarines though they seem to operate only on the surface. They are simply called *electrics*, and indeed the whole island is electrically run.

Earlier in his career Verne had written an historical story dealing with the Royalist rising, in Brittany, against the newly-formed Republican government. *Le Comte de Chantelaine, un Episode de la Révolution*, was serialized in *La Musée des Familles* in 1864 but never appeared in book form.

The 1880's saw great political unrest in France, and this induced him to write several books, mostly historical, whose theme is the fight for freedom. As was shown by *The Blockade Runners* and *The Mysterious Island*, in the American Civil War his sympathies had been with the North, and now he displayed them at greater length.

The hero of *North Against South* (1887) is a wealthy Abolitionist who owns a slave-run estate in Florida. Its villain is a rascal of Spanish origin who is known to be responsible for a number of crimes but who always escapes punishment through his incredible power of producing an alibi. At last he goads the estate-owner into freeing all his slaves, whereupon the authorities order all emancipated slaves to leave Florida.

When the slaves refuse to desert their master, the estate is attacked by a fanatical mob, and an attempt to send the threatened womenfolk into safety leads directly to the owner's small daughter being kidnapped by the scoundrel. Then he himself, with his son, is sentenced to death for being in treasonable communication with the Northern forces. In an exciting climax, the surprise ending consists of the explanation of the villain's extraordinary power of apparently being in two places at once. . . .

If it were suspected that Verne's scornful treatment of the negro servant in *The Clipper of the Clouds* meant that he was addicted to racial prejudice, *North against South* would exculpate him. The negroes who appear in the story are loyal and courageous, and its heroine is a devoted negress.

The Flight to France (1887), which suggests the influence of Erckmann-Chatrian, gives a vivid description of the Battle of Valmy. Its hero, a cavalry soldier, cares nothing for politics, his sole aim being to protect his country from invasion by the foreign counter-revolutionaries. He befriends a young conscript in the German army who, sentenced to death for striking a brutal officer, has escaped and is on the run. The two are captured and face a firing squad. . . .

One of Verne's pet aversions, what is now called the British 'Establishment', was intensified by the clash during the later part of the nineteenth century between the rival imperialisms of Britain and France.[1] Among his minor characters are some appalling English snobs and overbearing English officials, one of whom appears in the story of the wandering acrobats. César Cascabel so much detests the British because of our alleged ill-treatment of Napoleon, that while crossing British Columbia he refuses to give a performance; he will not soil his hands with English money. After some bullying aristocrat has refused to fight a duel with him because of his low social status, the Amazonian Madame Cascabel lays the culprit low with one swipe of her mighty hand!

The sufferings of the Irish peasants under English rule are exposed in *Foundling Mick* (1893). Its hero, an infant of three, undergoes varied hardships until he is adopted by some warm-hearted Irish peasants; he becomes one of the family until, unable after a bad season to pay their rent, they are brutally evicted and their home is demolished about their heads. Employed as a groom by a cold-hearted English nobleman, he is exposed to the tender mercies of his employer's loutish son.

This is not a 'hard luck story'. Far from it indeed; having relieved

[1] René Escaich.

his mind about the tyrannical English, Verne drops them, and the narrative becomes a 'success story' which in real life might have appeared in Samuel Smiles's *Self Help*. From peddling newspapers the child makes such progress that at an incredibly early age he is able to set up in business in Dublin as 'Little Boy & Co.', the 'Co.' consisting of an even younger waif whose life he had saved, and his faithful dog; needless to say, he also shows the heroism expected of a Verne hero. This story was well summed up by a schoolgirl who said that she liked books that made her cry but had got a happy ending. . . .

Verne's historical works are overshadowed by his adventure stories and his contributions to science fiction. One, because of its unusual plot, its original touch of humour, and its sincerity, deserves to be better known.

The subject of *A Family Without a Name* (1889) is one on which Verne felt strongly, the attempt, in 1837, of the French Canadians of Quebec to free themselves from British rule. The story opens with an earlier plot to arouse revolt by kidnapping the Province's Governor. The plot had been betrayed, and the name of the traitor, Simon Morgaz, has become a synonym for infamy.

The shame has descended upon his family, who devote their lives to expiating his treachery. His widow lives, or rather exists, in strictest seclusion, emerging only for works of piety or charity. Her eldest son, a priest, is spreading the flames of revolt with the fire of his sermons. Her younger son, known only as Jean-sans-Nom, is the soul of the Resistance Movement; he has won the love of one of its heroines, but how could he ask her to adopt the hated name of Morgaz?

This narrative, necessarily sombre, is enlivened by some admirable pen-pictures of life among the 'habitants' of Quebec, and by the inclusion of a law-abiding Quebec lawyer who sympathizes with the revolt but is determined to maintain the strictest neutrality. Not realizing that such a heritage may involve unexpected responsibilities, he takes an innocent pride in having Red Indian blood in his veins. This is not merely light relief, however, for unforeseeable consequences of his sudden accession to the chieftainship of a Huron tribe form a turning point in the revolt.

Verne lays stress on the brutalities of the English troops in quelling the rebellion; but at their worst these pale into insignificance compared with those of our own time, or, for that matter, with those of the Reign of Terror during the French Revolution.

There was no scope here for one of his favourite surprise endings, for the revolt is doomed to failure from the outset. Its first encouraging victory is soon overshadowed by a serious defeat, and events move forward inexorably to the last heroic stand of the Separatists on Navy Island, a little above Niagara Falls. The hapless mother dies of grief and shame; the elder brother perishes in circumstances recalling *A Tale of Two Cities*; and Jean-sans-Nom, realizing that his cause is hopeless but seeking to create a tradition that will inspire further revolts, is determined to fall in battle.

His end, in circumstances symbolic, Allott declares, of the ruthless British sweep forward to power, is so spectacular that one is amazed that it has never formed the climax of a film. Verne condemns the severity of the reprisals that followed the revolt but, with typical objectivity, points out that in the Dominion of Canada the status of the French Canadians has been greatly improved.

XV
Knotting up the Loose Ends

VERNE greatly disliked leaving 'loose ends' to his stories. *The Children of Captain Grant* had left uncertain the fate of a minor character, the mutineer Ayrton, marooned on a lonely island. More important, *Twenty Thousand Leagues* had left uncertain both the end and the very identity of Captain Nemo. Verne had already cleared up both these points in another of his *Strange Journeys.*

Towards the end of the century he knotted up several other loose ends to his earlier books. Now, however, he was writing in a very different spirit, so that the sequels to two of his masterpieces form only a regrettable anticlimax to the originals.

Anyone who loves the heroes of his Moon-travel stories will be distressed at the discomfiture they were to face. Not for all of those heroes, however—Verne could not have borne to heap contempt upon his old friend Nadar, and so Michel Ardan does not appear in *The Purchase of the North Pole* (1889), which might have been called *Topsy-Turvy.* Its French title is a complicated pun, for it might have been *Sens Dessus Dessous,* 'upside down', or *Sans Dessus ni Dessous,* 'with neither top nor bottom'. Instead Verne used the meaningless phrase *Sans Dessus Dessous* (he might just as well have written *C'en Dessus Dessous*) to convey not so much *renversement,* meaning 'inversion', as *bouleversement,* implying complete confusion.[1]

The book develops an idea glanced at in *From the Earth to the Moon.* Archimedes had declared that if he had a lever, and a place to stand on, he could move the earth, a feat which the Gun Club decide to accomplish in real earnest. Captain Nicholl has invented a super-explosive, and he and Barbicane propose to tunnel into the side of a mountain so as to produce a cannon firing a shot with so great a momentum that its reaction will tilt the earth's axis. This will make available for exploitation the mineral treasures buried beneath the Poles.

[1] Lamire and Moré.

J. T. Maston, again the venture's mathematician and back-room boy, is making his calculations on a blackboard when he is overthrown by a flash of lightning; though badly shaken, he carries on with his work. (In real life, the calculations were made by the mining engineer Alcide Badoureau; Verne was determined on accuracy, for the astronomer Flammarion had been making cutting remarks about 'the scientific inaccuracies of amateurs', and it was obvious whom he had in mind.)

Satisfied that the scheme is practicable, and financed by a widow who has fallen in love with Maston, Barbicane and Nicholl proceed. Callously indifferent to its unpredictable results, which may render much of the earth uninhabitable, they 'purchase the North Pole' (from whom is not clear) and excavate the giant cannon. The world is alarmed and the U.S. Government vetoes the project, but what can be done? Barbicane and Nicholl are in hiding and Maston, who has been jailed, refuses to divulge the mountain's position.

The panic intensifies as 'zero hour' approaches. But nothing happens; when the cannon is fired, the projectile, presumably solid and unaimed, cleaves the air with a 'frightful shriek', but the earth is unmoved. The public relief gives way to ridicule, especially when a French mathematician explains that Maston had made a preposterous mistake in his calculations; the lightning had so confused him that he had grossly underestimated the earth's mass! Disillusioned, the poor fellow abjures mathematics but finds consolation in his marriage with the benevolent widow. . . .

The narrative shows Verne's growing uneasiness about the progress of materialistic science. This came to a climax shortly before his death in his sequel to *The Clipper of the Clouds*.

In *The Purchase of the North Pole* he had merely ridiculed the characters whom he had formerly loved; far more dreadful is the fate he reserves for Robur. At the end of the earlier book he had represented him as a symbolic figure with a certain nobility:

> 'Who is this Robur? Shall we ever know. . . . Robur is the science of the future, perhaps that of tomorrow. He is the forerunner of what is to come.'

Robur himself, as his final words show, had realized the evil possibilities of science:

'"Citizens of the United States . . . I go; and I take my secret with me. But it shall not be lost to humanity. It shall belong to you on the day when you are educated enough to profit from it and wise enough not to misuse it. Farewell!"'

In *Master of the World* (1904) these qualities have vanished. Robur has now perfected an invention even more remarkable than his helicopter, a combined racing-car, submarine, and ornithopter. With it he means to dominate mankind; once so voluble, he now hardly speaks, preferring to issue threatening manifestoes. His invention, the *Terrible* (Épouvantable—'frightful' would be a more accurate translation), will, he declares, give him 'complete power over the whole world', which no human strength can withstand.

He has become almost inhuman, an embodiment of evil like the incarnate Antichrist of Monsignor Robert Hugh Benson's *Lord of the World* and the disembodied Head of the National Institute of Co-ordinated Experiment in C. S. Lewis's *That Hideous Strength.*

Though no human strength can withstand him, there is a Power that can. When he deliberately flies into the heart of an electrical storm, a blasphemous challenge on his lips, 'I—Robur—Robur—Master of the World', the *Épouvantable* is struck by lightning 'stroke upon stroke', and its shattered fragments are hurled to earth. Thus Robur meets the same fate as Master Zacharius; Verne was ending just as he had begun, as indeed he had always been, a devout Christian who honoured science but only in its proper place.

The loose ends he tied up were not only those of his own books.[1] *Propeller Island* had fulfilled his childish dream of the Ile Feydeau's putting out to sea. Another of his books was suggested by his memories of his teacher in the dame school, Mme Samblain, with her faith that her husband who had sailed away into the unknown so soon after their marriage would one day return. He was still, moreover, as much impressed as when he had written *The English at the North Pole* with the repeated attempts which Lady Franklin had made to rescue her lost husband.

He was far too good an artist to make fiction follow fact slavishly, so that the heroine who gives her name to *Mrs Branican* (1891) sees her husband sail away not immediately after their marriage but

[1] It has been suggested that he completed Dickens's unfinished story, *The Mystery of Edwin Drood*, but I have been unable to find any confirmation of this.

shortly after the birth of their first child. Nor does he merely fail to return; his vessel is reported as definitely lost with all hands. Hot on this news comes a blow which fells her: her child is swept from her arms by a wave and drowned.

Her reason lost, she is cared for first by her brother-in-law, a plausible villain, and then by a friendly ship-owner. On regaining her sanity she refuses to believe in her husband's death, and, like Lady Franklin, she sends a rescue expedition to search for him. All it brings back is a confirmation of his fate.

Her faithfulness to his memory is rewarded when years later tidings come that he may still be alive. No longer content to send out a rescue expedition, she insists on heading it herself.

Later she is joined by a youth whose features recall her husband's, and whose spontaneous affection she reciprocates. Yet he cannot, as the reader might suspect, be the son whose loss she mourned, for that child's body had been found and buried. . . . Complications arise from the reappearance of the scoundrelly brother-in-law and his downtrodden wife, and light relief is gained from a comic Englishman who collects celebrated hats and is searching among the savages for the most famous article of headgear in history. . . .

Verne thought that *The Swiss Family Robinson*, which had so much influenced him, was incomplete, though he was probably the only one of its readers to notice this. He set himself to remedy this defect in *Second Fatherland* (1900—its English translation formed two volumes, *Their Island Home and The Castaways of the 'Flag'*). In a foreword he makes clear his indebtedness to its author, J. R. Wyss, and to Defoe:

> 'The Robinsons were the books of my childhood and they have remained with me as a permanent memory. Frequent reading has only strengthened their appeal, and I have not recaptured in any modern books the impressions of my first youth. Certainly my passion for these adventure-stories instinctively put me on the path I was to follow.'

It was for this reason, he adds, that he wrote his own desert island stories, 'a very close relation to those of Defoe and Wyss'.

Wyss leaves most of his Swiss Family comfortably settled on a small portion of the island, the only part they had troubled to explore. Verne's sequel remedies this defect; the islanders not only begin a systematic exploration of their home but start mechanizing it, excavating a canal and constructing a pumping-engine worked by a waterwheel. Having ascended a mountain, they fly on its summit the British flag.

The Castaways referred to in the second English title are some members of the family who are returning from a visit to the outer world when there is a mutiny. Turned adrift in a small boat with a few seamen, they land on an unknown shore where they meet with varied adventures: what this has to do with the rest of the family is not made clear until the end of the story. This suggests that to Verne's mind no such narrative was complete until the desert island had been incorporated into the British Empire!

There is no doubt about the incompleteness of the other story which Verne undertook to finish; it is cut short with a surgical abruptness. *The Narrative of Arthur Gordon Pym of Nantucket* is the very strangest work of that very strange writer Edgar Allan Poe, and there is no wonder that it so much impressed Verne.

Pym, the story's narrator, stows himself away, only to find that his vessel has been captured by mutineers and that he himself is in the direst peril. Saved by a friendly member of the crew, he and his companion are able to turn the tables on the mutineers, but are themselves starved into cannibalism.

He and Peters are picked up by a British ship trading in the South Seas, the *Jane Guy*. Partly at Pym's instigation her captain, William Guy, pushes on into the unknown Antarctic, where they encounter conditions suggestive of the unearthly worlds of science fiction. The carcase of a strange animal is found floating in the sea; the vessel reaches some islands where the rocks, the vegetation, and even the water of the streams have bizarre properties: great chasms in the hills spell out a cryptic message; the inhabitants are human but their teeth are black, and they evince a panic-terror at the sight of anything white.

At first friendly, the natives turn without warning on their visitors and massacre them. Pym and Peters, the only survivors, escape in a native boat into the unknown and a current sweeps them towards the Pole.

Now science fiction passes into fantasy. A light grey vapour, shot with the flashes of the Aurora, appears in the south; the sea becomes warm and then hot and resembles milk; its movements are responsive to flickerings in the vapour. A white powder falls from the sky, and the vapour, which now covers the whole southern horizon, looks like an immense cataract rolling down from on high; in its rents appear 'flitting indistinct images'.

Now Pym may be allowed to speak for himself:

> 'The darkness had materially increased, relieved only by the glare of the water thrown back from the white curtain before us. Many gigantic and pallidly white birds flew continuously now from before the veil . . . and now we rushed into the embrace of the cataract, where a chasm threw itself open to receive us. But there arose in our pathway a shrouded human figure, very far larger in its proportions than any dweller among men. And the hue of the skin of the figure was of the perfect whiteness of the snow.'

Here cryptically and disappointingly, the *Narrative* ends, and the mystery of that shrouded figure remains undisclosed. Yan Dargent, who illustrated Verne's critique of Poe in the *Musée*, depicts it as the Angel of Death, scythe uplifted to menace the castaways as they cower in the boat. Verne, when he wrote this article in 1864, took a less tragic view:

> 'Still, we have to believe that Gordon Pym got out of it because he himself produced this strange narrative; but he died before having completed his work. Poe seems to have deeply regretted this, and to have declined the task of filling in the gap.'

Of the attempts which have been made to explain 'this strange narrative', that most generally accepted is well summed up by Basil Ashmore in his Introduction to *The Mystery of Arthur Gordon Pym* in the Fitzroy Edition of Jules Verne.

In this view, supported by the similarity in rhythm between the two names, Pym is a personification of Poe himself and the whole story is allegorical. Pym sweeping towards the towering figure is Poe being borne down to death, so how could he complete the story of a journey he was yet to make?

There are other possibilities. Poe might have been retelling a nightmare, the story ending when he woke up. Or he may have got into such a tangle that he had no idea how to finish it, and had to cut it short.

If Poe himself could not unravel the tangle he had woven, nobody else could be expected to, so that Verne can hardly be blamed for dismissing some of its more bizarre features as being simply due to hallucination. Retaining those incidents which suited him, he re-wove them into a remarkable narrative.

The Sphinx of the Ice-fields (1897) represents William Guy's brother Len Guy as being convinced that the former has survived and as going out in search of him. One of his crew proves to be Pym's companion Dirk Peters; the two had been separated, and he had returned to America with Pym's diary. Poe had embellished and fictionalized this beyond all reason; of that 'shrouded human figure', for example, Peters knows nothing.

Guided by an apparently chance discovery, Len Guy pushes on in his brother's track, the hazards and encounters he experiences being complicated by the sudden revelation that among his crew is the brother of the seaman whom Dirk Peters and Pym had slain and eaten.

Conditions in the Far South were then unknown, and Verne was quite justified in representing the Antarctic Continent as being cleft by a channel, the Jane Strait; it was on the shore of this that Captain Nemo had located the South Pole. During the summer this channel is free from ice, and in it the adventurers encounter phenomena 'as extraordinary as those described by Arthur Pym'. At last they are swept along to that vaguely seen form which gives its title to Verne's story, *The Sphinx of the Ice-fields*, excellent both as a sequel to Poe's strange narrative and as a masterpiece of science fiction in its own right.

XVI
Controverted Questions

DURING the eighteen-nineties Verne showed signs of flagging; many—by no means all—of the stories he produced were very poor, the mass-produced products of a 'driven' pen. 'Words will not come to me' he was heard to complain, but whether they came or not he continued to write, and presently they returned. A few comments on his second-raters may form a prelude to the controversies which his work aroused.

Claudius Bombarnac (1893) is a belated by-product of *Around the World.* The Trans-Siberian Railway, work on which had begun, would of course allow globe-trotting to be completed in far less than the traditional eighty days, but Verne pointed out that this route, being further from the Equator than that followed by Fogg, would be much shorter, and he acidly commented that the feat would become a mere matter of being carried round passively in a comfortable seat.[1]

Bombarnac is a journalist sent to report on a journey from Asia Minor to China on the newly-opened (and imaginary) 'Trans-Asiatic Railway'. The train carries a consignment of gold, and this, though in theory a secret, has been so well-publicized in the European Press that the bandits of Asia are out to intercept it. . . .

The opening of *Captain Antifer* (1894) recalls that of *The Children of Captain Grant.* A French seaman is joint-heir to a pirate hoard, but all he knows is its latitude, and not for some years does the other heir turn up with the longitude. When after some by-play they reach the assigned spot, all they find is a direction to another spot miles away, and this again yields nothing but the latitude of yet a third; for its longitude they are referred to an austere Scots minister who point-blank refuses to co-operate in this quest for filthy lucre. When the information he (literally) bears comes to light, the gold-hunters reach the given spot, only to find some cryptic directions to the place where the treasure had actually been concealed. . . .

[1] Marcel Hutin in *L'Echo de Paris*, quoted by Lamire.

The central character in *Clovis Dardentor* (1896), which Verne called an 'unrhymed variety show' (*vaudeville sans couplets*), is a wealthy childless man who wants to adopt an heir. Two young candidates realize that for the adoption to be legal they have first to save their sponsor's life, and their efforts to rescue him from flood, fire fang, during a journey across the Mediterranean into Algeria, provide the story's main episodes. Results are not at all what they anticipate. . . .

It was when Verne based *The Superb Oronoco* (1898) on material supplied by the French explorer Jean Chaffanjon that his English publishers, who had hitherto produced almost everything he wrote, began to discriminate: thenceforth they published only about half-a-dozen of the score or so of his later works and this was not one of them. They can hardly be blamed: it is a long and laboured account of an expedition sent to discover the true course of that unexplored South American river, and though it includes some exciting episodes it is not very interesting. . . .

The Will of an Eccentric (1899) bequeaths a fortune to whichever of the possible heirs can most quickly reach a number of points, chosen at random, in the United States; the surprise ending shows the interest in catalepsy which Verne had gained from Poe. The original edition had what would now be called a 'gimmick', a game, played with dice on a board, based on the story.

The Yarns of Jean-Marie Cabidoulin (1901) is as long-winded as its title suggests, and its re-naming as *The Sea-Serpent* made it no more enticing. Its hero discourses at great length on his objections to again going to sea, and apart from a rather exciting ending that is about all.

Of all Verne's multifarious productions, *Travelling Scholarship* (1903) is the worst; the award, made to some brilliant French students, is a tour of the Antilles. What little interest the story has is swamped in the mass of geographical information.

The theme of *The Invasion of the Sea* (1905) is the excavation of a channel from the Mediterranean into one of the great depressions, below sea-level, in the Sahara; round the inland sea thus formed the desert might be transformed into a fertile countryside with flourishing villages and towns. The nomadic tribes of the region combine in an effort to thwart the project. . . .

It may have been the promising title *The Lighthouse at the End of the World* (1905) which led Verne's English publishers to produce a translation. The plot, the erection of a lighthouse on the tip of Cape Horn and the attack upon it of a horde of pirates, would have made a good short, or long-short, story, but is too slight to justify a full-length book. . . .

These dull long-winded efforts were interspersed with some really brilliant work, and this contrast, combined with their author's secluded life, led to rumours that Verne had given up writing, and that the narratives which bore his name were really the output of a syndicate of 'ghosts', *Jules Verne et Cie*. He himself cared nothing for this, but so widely did the rumour spread, so much disquiet did it arouse in the literary world, that the Italian critic Edmondo de Amicis made a special visit to Amiens to enquire into it.

Nobody likes having it hinted, however delicately, that he is suspected of perpetrating a fraud on the public, so it is not surprising that at first Verne received him rather coldly. But, melted by his visitor's charm and tact, he took him into his study and showed him his works of reference and three manuscripts in various stages of completion. When De Amicis explained that people were doubting that one person could possibly write so much, Honorine protested that her husband was killing himself with work, but Verne declared that when he was not working he did not really feel alive.

The visit so much aroused him from his sedentary habits that he showed his visitor the sights of Amiens and took him into a café which, Honorine commented, they had not entered for years; Verne seems to have been cheered by this unusual break in his daily routine. Armed with a signed photograph, to show that there really was such a person, De Amicis returned to Italy, to reassure the literary world that there was no spurious *Jules Verne et Cie* but simply the one and only Jules Verne, the undoubted author of all the works bearing his name.

(It is I suppose conceivable that some of Verne's posthumous works were completed by other hands, but there is no evidence of anything more than legitimate editing.)

While this controversy was being settled, another had dragged Verne into the law courts. In 1894 he had explained to his brother Paul an idea he had in mind for a combined submarine, surface vessel and aircraft; its inventor would be not another Captain Nemo but 'half a nobleman and half a scoundrel', and there might be a spy on board. How the story would end he had no idea, but the vessel might blockade the Mediterranean by setting nets across the Straits of Gibraltar.

It seems a pity that so promising an idea was never used, but it produced two separate stories. One, *Master of the World*, has already been considered; the other was based on a widely publicized episode.

A brilliant but slightly unbalanced French chemist, Eugène Turpin, had invented the explosive melinite, based, like the British lyddite, on picric acid. The French Government rejected it, whereupon its inventor attacked the authorities in a book so virulent that the British Museum Library Catalogue described it as having been banned.

Whether Verne had Turpin in mind or not, this episode may have helped to suggest his story *For the Flag* (1896). In this a French inventor, Thomas Roch, has literally been driven insane by the rejection of his explosive, the Fulgurator, not only by his own government but by several others. Interned in an American nursing home, he is watched over by his male nurse, Simon Hart, a French chemist who believes that the Fulgurator is genuine and hopes to reveal its secret to his government.

There is someone else who believes in the Fulgurator: the Count d'Artigas, of whom little is known except that he is a wealthy yachtsman, believed to hail from Malaya or Indonesia. Having kidnapped Roch and Hart, he takes them to sea on his yacht; but when she is intercepted and searched by the United States authorities there is no sign that either has ever been on board.

When Hart is released from what seems like a prison cell, he finds however that both Roch and himself are actually on the yacht. Though her sails are furled, though she has no funnel and no visible means of propulsion, she is moving through the waters at high speed. . . .

Here there is the 'half nobleman and half scoundrel' that Verne had in mind, for the Count is really the fierce pirate Ker Kerraje. By working on the one emotion left to the distraught inventor, that of hate, he hopes to use the Fulgurator to destroy any force sent to attack his lair. Is there nothing that Hart can do to thwart him? Can he get no word to civilization of this dastardly plot? Is there no hope that the embittered inventor, who has rejected all notions of patriotism, may have vestiges of a better nature to which he might appeal? . . .

Convinced that the Thomas Roch of the narrative was meant for himself, Turpin, instead of wisely keeping silent in the hope that nobody else would think so, brought an action against the author for defamation of character. Defended by one of his admirers, the brilliant young advocate Raymond Poincaré, Verne won his case, as he did when it went to appeal. The only results of the trial were that it gave the book greater publicity, that it may have confirmed the impression that Roch was really meant for Turpin, and that, much against his will, it took Verne to Paris. Now he could no longer declare, as he had hitherto done, that the reason for his promotion[1] to Officer in the Legion of Honour was that he was the only Frenchman in France who had never seen the Eiffel Tower!

Of all the accusations launched against Verne, the most serious was the suggestion that he was not really the author of *Twenty Thousand Leagues Under the Sea,* but that he had purchased the manuscript for a mere hundred francs (about 75s.) from Louise Michel, and that she, although she was starving, had spent the purchase price not on herself but on the needy poor.

The fact behind this fiction was more trivial even than that behind the Polish Jew story. Louise Michel, whose heroism during the Commune and whose moral integrity and benevolence had earned her the name of the Red Virgin, had been sentenced to the penal settlements in New Caledonia. During her imprisonment she had seen a mollusc, the pearly nautilus, and her description of it was said to have been the first ever written—though the animal had in fact long been known to science. From the misstatement that Verne had learned about the nautilus (the mollusc) from her it was easy to jump to the conclusion that this was the *Nautilus* (the submarine); such picturesque details as the beggarly price, the heroine's starvation, and the generous gift to the poor were still easier to add.

The whole legend was discredited—one might almost say debunked—in 1959 by the Belgian critic Hem Day.[2] Cyrille Andreev, in his Preface to the Russian edition of Verne's works,[3] does not even refer to it, though if there were any doubt about the book's author-

[1] In 1892, on the recommendation of the *Maire* of Amiens.

[2] Hem Day, *Louise Michel—Jules Verne: De qui est '20,000 Lieues sous les Mers'?*

[3] Quoted in *Europe*, April/May 1955.

ship he might have been expected to give its benefit to the Communard Louise Michel rather than to the bourgeois Jules Verne. He takes the view that right from the outset Verne had meant *The Children of Captain Grant, 20,000 Leagues under the Sea* and *The Mysterious Island* to form a trilogy; I do not think this view is justified, but it is flatly inconsistent with the Louise Michel story.

What is more, *20,000 Leagues* reads not like Louise Michel, but like Verne; the original idea for the story has also been attributed to George Sand; and it is further said that he hit upon it when discussing the laying of the Transatlantic cable with the seamen of the *Great Eastern*![1]

My own opinion is that though he may have discussed it both with Louise Michel and with George Sand, and he no doubt derived useful information from his discussion with the *Great Eastern*'s seamen, the idea was certainly his own. *A Voyage Beneath the Waters* was a natural sequel to the journeys through the air across Africa and across the ice to the North Pole, down a volcanic crater into the bowels of the earth, and beyond the atmosphere around the moon. He probably had it in mind as one of his *Strange Journeys* right from the outset.

A more intimate question was suggested by another of Verne's narratives. Early in the nineties he had suffered from a mood of depression so intense that it alarmed his family. Mme de la Fuye suggests that the 'amplified memory of a secret and perhaps wholly intellectual passion' is to be found in *Carpathian Castle* (1892).

Whether there is anything in her suggestion readers of this remarkable narrative can judge for themselves. Does the tragic end of its heroine really symbolize some emotional crisis in Verne's own life, the loss perhaps of someone who he had secretly loved but who, as a married man, he could never hope to win? Or did he compose it, as I am tempted to suspect, with his tongue in his cheek? It would be like Jules Verne to write a story because his heart was breaking and then to laugh at himself for doing it.

The heroine, La Stilla, is a famous opera-singer about to retire from the stage because of some unknown admirer who attends every one of her performances; he does not seek to molest her in any way, and she never even sees him, but the knowledge that he is always there, unseen behind the curtains of his box, tells on her nerves. As

[1] Gilette Ziegler, *Jules Verne 1828–1905*.

on the eve of her marriage she is giving her farewell performance, he suddenly appears just as she is striving for a top note. Combined with that artistic effort, the sight of his remarkable countenance so unnerves her that she drops dead upon the stage![1]

Admittedly *Carpathian Castle* is unique among Verne's narratives, but that to my mind is simply because he was deliberately reviving an obsolete art-form. The 'Gothic story' was the thriller of the eighteenth century: its scenery was evocative, wild mountains or forests and picturesque ruins; its characters were gloomy noblemen, simple peasants, faithful serving-men, and distressed heroines; and it abounded in apparently supernatural phenomena, inexplicable voices, gleaming lights ('We saw enough of them', Jane Austen comments, 'to make a respectable illumination') and flitting figures in white. For most of the authors it was a point of honour to end the book with a matter-of-fact explanation of such phenomena, but this, as Sir Walter Scott put it, could be as incredible as the phenomena themselves.

The scene of Verne's narrative is that home of the werewolf and vampire, the Balkans. Here, to the terror of the peasants, smoke is seen rising from a castle known to be empty and reputed to be under a curse. Undeterred by a disembodied voice which warns him to keep away, a gallant young forester tries to enter the castle, only to be inexplicably hurled away in agony as he lays hands on its walls, while his companion is for a time rooted, just as inexplicably, to the ground.

A young nobleman, the bereaved lover of the ill-fated La Stilla, happens to visit the neighbourhood. He hears her voice echoing in his ear; he sees her white-clad form on the castle's battlements; the drawbridge is lowered and the portal stands open to admit him, but hardly does he enter than the one rises, and the other closes, to cut off his retreat.

Being couched in terms of science fiction, the matter-of-fact explanation is less incredible than usual. That unknown admirer of La Stilla, the man whose sudden appearance had brought about her death, blames for her loss the nobleman who was to have married her, and who has employed a brilliant scientist to devise some means of luring him into the castle.

[1] An episode perhaps suggested by the tragic death of Edgar Allan Poe's young wife.

XVII
Minor Works

TOWARDS Verne's sixtieth year his thoughts, to judge by two of his shorter works, were turning back towards his childhood. They appeared respectively in the *Figaro Illustré* for January 1891 and—appropriately, for the climax of the second story is set at Christmas—December 1893.

In spite of his disability and his dislike of travel, in 1887 he visited Liége[1] to read to the Société d'Emulation his fantasy, *The Adventures of the Rat Family*. A synopsis will enable the reader to judge whether he meant it as a real fairy story for the delight of children or as a burlesque for the entertainment of sardonic adults.

All the traditional figures appear, the wicked enchanter and the good fairy, the evil prince who wants to marry the charming heroine, and the gallant young hero who truly loves her. But the magician is a bungler, the good fairy is either absent-minded or slightly incompetent, and, though the villain is human, the heroine is a member of an engaging family of rats. The story is based on the theory of metempsychosis, which, even though Verne explains it, is a bit of a mouthful for children. Thanks partly to the ineptitude of the enchanter, but chiefly to the somewhat inefficient benevolence of the good fairy, the Rat Family, after passing through various intermediate stages, becomes human—but with the heroine's cousin afflicted for life with a donkey's tail!

The hero and heroine of *Mr Ray Sharp and Miss Me Flat*, the only Verne story whose principal characters are children, are named after what one of their elders calls their 'physiological notes'. He and his assistant are weird Hoffmanesque personages who suddenly enter a remote Swiss village (period not stated) and undertake to tune and amplify the church organ and to train the children who form the village choir. Each child, he explains, has an individual 'natural note', the only one which he or she should sing, and he arranges them in order of their place in the musical scale, as though they

[1] Escaich and Moré.

were a set of human organ pipes, with quite disconcerting results. . . .

This fantasy may have been suggested by its author's impending deafness and shows that his love of music included an interest in its theory. An essential point in the narrative is the difference, imperceptible to any ear except a musician's, between the two notes proper to the hero and the heroine.

Both these stories formed part of the French edition of *Yesterday and Tomorrow.* Like *The Humbug, The Rat Family* has been excluded from the English version as lacking in interest, several of Verne's shorter pieces being substituted. These were not published separately but were included with the original editions, though not with the English translations, of three of the *Strange Travels.*

Included with *The Lottery Ticket, Fritt-Flacc* is a horror story probably suggested by Poe's *William Wilson.* A mercenary doctor, living amid 'Gothic story' surroundings, is suddenly called upon to heal his double. . . .

In *Gil Braltar,* which appeared with *The Flight to France,* Verne makes merry at the expense of his bugbear, the British 'Establishment'. Its hero, a half-crazed hidalgo, is convinced that his name marks him out as destined to free Gibraltar from the British and to restore it to Spain. Endowed with a strange influence over animals, he leads the well-known Gibraltar apes in a surprise attack upon the garrison of 'the Rock'. How can the British commander cope with such an invasion? . . .

Verne was as cold to hunting as he was to fishing. When his family, concerned for his health and thinking he needed exercise, invited him to go duck-shooting, he simply reminded them that the only thing he had ever brought down, in 1859, was a gendarme's hat, and that he would let it go at that.

This episode, factual or otherwise, is described in a paper, *Ten Hours' Hunting,* which he read to the Academy of Amiens; it was published in their *Memoirs* for 1881 and reprinted with the French edition of *The Green Ray.* Although his biographers seem to have taken quite seriously this sardonic account of the mishaps he claimed to have suffered during a shooting expedition, to my mind it was the mere flight of fancy (*simple boutade*) which he called it, and had no more solid backing than his alleged dream about Amiens of the future!

An historical episode which was certain to appeal to Jules Verne because of its desert island theme is briefly described in his only 'documentary', *The Mutineers of the 'Bounty'*. It appeared both in the French and, translated by W. H. G. Kingston, in the original English, versions of *The Begum's Fortune*.[1] While giving it added vividness by imagined conversations, Verne explains in a footnote:

> 'We think it well to inform our readers that this narrative is in no way fictional; all its details are taken from the maritime annals of Great Britain. Reality provides us with facts so romantic that imagination itself could add nothing to them.'

Though Verne had begun his career as a dramatist, that was not his real vocation, and apart from *Around the World* and *Michael Strogoff*, none of his plays was a success. Even d'Ennery could not do anything with *The Children of Captain Grant*, though in 1878 he tried to liven it up with some tasteless comedy and though its ending, in which a child's death-bed moves a hardened criminal to repentance, is a real tear-jerker. To bring on to the stage a whale-hunt and a vessel burning and blowing up baffled even his talents; what he really needed was the cinema-screen.

Verne must have regarded without overmuch enthusiasm another of d'Ennery's efforts in 1882 to adapt his work for the stage. His *Journey through the Impossible* is described as:

> 'A sort of scenic résumé of the *Strange Journeys* in which there intermingle, perhaps somewhat astonished to find themselves together, some of the personages of the inventive narrator. Dr Ox, Captain Nemo, the son of Captain Hatteras and so forth. It is moreover a strange marriage of two minds: even while he exploits Jules Verne's anecdotes not too happily, d'Ennery, elderly and morose, does not trouble to conceal his disdain for all the recent achievements, and describes the work of the courageous modern scientists as "infamous".[2]

A short story, ascribed to Jules Verne and Charles Wallut, *The Adopted Son*, has the same general theme as *Clovis Dardentor*.

[1] It is *not* included in the Fitzroy Edition, either of *The Begum's Fortune* or of *Yesterday and Tomorrow*.

[2] Paul Ginisty in *La Féerie*, quoted by Escaich.

Though never printed, it was broadcast in 1950 by La Radiodiffusion Française.[1]

One or two of Verne's minor works have never come into print: an untitled story; *Journey through England and Scotland*; *Paris in the Twentieth Century*. 'Why weren't they published?' asks Escaich. 'Were they left incomplete? Don't they offer much interest? One would like to know.' Or was it, as he suggests, that Verne's writing, 'very fine and cramped and difficult to decipher', might have made them illegible?

This suggests a note on Verne's method of work, which he described in an interview with Mrs Marie A. Belloc:[2]

> 'I start by making a draft of a new story. I never begin without knowing what the beginning, middle, and end will be. I have always been fortunate to have not one but half a dozen definite schemes in mind. If I ever find myself hard up for a subject, I shall consider it time for me to give up work. After completing a preliminary draft I draw up a plan of the chapters; then I begin the actual writing of the first rough copy in pencil, leaving a half-page margin for corrections and emendations; I then read the whole and go over all I have already done in ink. I consider my real labour begins with my first set of proofs, for I not only correct something in every sentence but I rewrite whole chapters. I do not seem to have a grip of my subject till I see my work in print; fortunately my kind publisher allows me every latitude as regards corrections, and I also have as many as eight or ten revises. I envy but do not attempt to emulate the example of those who, from the time they write chapter I to the word *Finis*, never see reason to alter or add a single word.'

He did, however, revise some of his works after they had been serialized but before they appeared as books. He might have discovered new facts to add to them, as he had done with the sub-human monster in *Journey to the Centre of the Earth*. Or he might want to make some episode more effective: only in the book versions does *Master Zacharius* refuse to bow at the most sacred moment of the Mass, or Captain Hatteras become reconciled with his American rival in their quest for the North Pole.

[1] René Escaich.

[2] *Strand Magazine*, February 1895.

Several stories, published under other names or anonymously, have been doubtfully attributed to Verne. Four appeared in Czarist Russia.[1] Edmondo Marcucci mentions as almost unobtainable several published not in France but in Italy under Verne's name. He adds that *A Mexican Vendetta* might be a translation of *A Drama in Mexico*, but that *Darius the Corsair*, an incident in the war waged by the privateers against Britain in 1814, is full of vulgarisms and absolutely inconsistent with Verne's style and spirit.[2]

Another, *A Nightmare*, could be a translation of a French book. This appeared under the authorship of X. Nagrien (1869), as did *A Prodigious Discovery and its incalculable Consequences for the Future* (1867—both published by Hetzel). Escaich regards both as the work of Verne, having many of his characteristics in the style, the composition, the vigour, the care about details; and he suggests that the reason for the pseudonym was simply that the *Prodigious Discovery* 'belongs to the realm of pure fantasy, devoid of any scientific basis and out of keeping with all Verne's other work'.

Admittedly there is a suggestion of the Vernian love for puns in the pseudonym: 'X' might stand not, as the story declares, for 'Xavier' but for the algebraic unknown quantity, and 'Nagrien' explained as being a contraction of 'NAviGator aeRIEN', also includes the word *rien*, 'nothing'. Nevertheless, I still feel doubtful about the book's authorship and again a synopsis may help the reader to judge.

Mr X, as he might be called, has invented a way of increasing, reversing, or nullifying gravity. Suspended from a tiny gadget, he is thus able to soar, to the amazement of all beholders, above Paris and to perch on the topmost pinnacle of Notre Dame. Using a larger contrivance he takes a shipload of notabilities on a cruise over France, and then embarks on a flight round the world. But, as he declares in a letter smuggled out at great expense to a sympathetic newspaper, this was cut short near Vienna. Fearing the loss of their trade, the railway interests have interned him in a great building among madmen. Here agents of the railways, disguised as doctors or keepers, keep trying to persuade him that he never made any such discovery or flight, and that the very paper whose help he is seeking does not exist at all.

[1] Correspondence from Svante Kjellberg, of Sweden.

[2] Quoted by Escaich.

Verne would not have been a French *littérateur* if he had not written poetry. Examples of this are included as Appendices to the Fitzroy Edition of *Black Diamonds, The Tribulations of a Chinese Gentleman,* Part I of *The Fur Country,* and *A Family without a Name*; translations of the last three appear in the text. That in the last-named, *Will-of-the-Wisp,* is especially good in both its French and English versions; I regret that I have been unable to find the name of its translator.

XVIII
Final Achievements

VERNE, who liked keeping well ahead of schedule and often had two or three books going at once, was not discouraged by the realization that some could not be published until after his death. Perhaps because of the First World War, most of his posthumous and other late works did not appear in England until recently; a pity, for almost all are interesting and some excellent.

How many of his British readers, for example, realize that he experimented with detective stories? Though not good of their kind, their plots are original and they show his versatility and his love for freedom. Considering his admiration for Poe, whose *Rue Morgue* and *Purloined Letter* he had praised highly, this is not surprising: moreover, even in the unlikely event of his being ignorant of Sherlock Holmes, he was a compatriot of those pioneers of the *roman policier*, Vidocq and Gaboriau, and detectives figure in *Around the World, A Family Without a Name*, and *Master of the World. The Children of Captain Grant*, moreover, might have won the approval of the Crime Club itself, with its careful attention to detail, its 'red herrings', and its essential clue given, but cunningly concealed, right at the outset.

In *A Livonian Drama* (1904) a bank clerk is murdered and robbed. Suspicion naturally falls on a 'mystery man' who has travelled with him and stayed at the same inn but had spoken hardly a word and had kept his face hidden. Is he the culprit? Or, as the clash of races in the Baltic States forms a background to the story, could he be a political fugitive trying to evade the frontier guards? . . .

The Danube Plot (1908) will have a special appeal to anglers. The winner of a competition held by a Danubian Fisherman's Society is an obscure member whose face is partly concealed by blue glasses. His colleagues welcome his offer to set up a world's record by living on the proceeds of his daily catch as he cruises down the Danube to the Black Sea.

He is in fact the leader of an underground movement against Turkish domination and this is his ingenious way of averting suspicion. But the local chief of police suspects him of being the leader of a gang of bandits, and the bandits suspect him of being the chief of police! Escaping from imprisonment by the one, he falls straight into the hands of the other. . . .

Though involving a murder mystery, *The Kip Brothers* (1902) is not so much a detective story as one of the yarns of mutiny which always appealed to Verne. During a profitable trading venture in the South Seas, two treacherous seamen rob and murder their captain, and suspicion falls on two brothers, Karl and Pieter Kip. Condemned to the penal settlements in Tasmania—among some Irish Fenians whom Verne, with his uncritical sympathy for rebels against British rule, regards as idealistic patriots—they escape. Then a photograph of the murdered man is examined with a powerful lens.

Verne now makes dramatic use, worthy of Poe, of a time-honoured superstition,[1] for visible upon the dead man's eyes are the last things he beheld at the moment of death. There, 'appearing in all their ferocity', are the faces of his two murderers!

The scene of Verne's historical story, *The Secret of Wilhelm Storitz* (1910), is an eighteenth-century Hungarian town. Here Storitz, a sinister German scientist, has inherited from his father, a famous alchemist who flourished when alchemy was being converted into chemistry, a secret which gives him an inexplicable power, bordering on magic, of persecuting undetected a respectable family and of terrorizing a whole community. In coping with this unprecedented problem the local Chief of Police displays an astounding virtuosity. . . .

Perhaps it was as light relief after these rather grim stories that Verne wrote *The Thompson Travel Agency* (1907), describing the misadventures of a party of sightseers on a pleasure cruise to the islands in the Atlantic. In competing with a rival Agency, its incompetent organizer has cut the fare down ruinously, recouping himself by economizing in everything, from the quality of the food to the seaworthiness of his vessel and the efficiency of her engines.

Among the trippers are some snobbish English aristocrats, a rascally American fortune-seeker, a chronic drunkard, an inveterate fault-finder, and two husband-hunting old maids; their father, a

[1] Suggested, according to Moré, from an episode in *Claire Lenoir* by Villiers de l'Isle Adam.

retired grocer, recalls Molière's M. Jourdain. In contrast with these are the two charming American heroines and the two debonair French heroes, as well as the courageous and efficient captain and crew. The narrative deals less with adventures and more with personal character than most of Verne's stories, but it ends excitingly.

Fascinated as he always was by developments in science, Verne was bound to be interested in the Theory of Evolution. Discussing with a journalist a book he was writing, he explained that it was based on the somewhat inconclusive attempts made by an American professor, Dr Garnier, to learn the language of the apes, and added:

> 'I am trying to reconstruct a race intermediate between the most advanced of the apes and the lowest men. . . . I deal with the question broadly and fancifully, and, anyhow, I am far from reaching the same conclusion as Darwin, whose ideas I do not share at all.'

The book appeared as *Le Village Aérien* (1901), but to avoid giving the impression that it dealt with some sort of flying-machine, its English translation is called *The Village in the Treetops*. While two elephant-hunters are descending a river through the unexplored African bush, a young native who accompanies them rescues a strange creature: though it resembles a young ape, it utters an articulate word!

Kinsmen of this enigmatic creature rescue it and the travellers from drowning and welcome them to their village, built on a huge framework secured to the upper branches of the trees. Here, apart from thoughts of escaping, the chief preoccupation of the hunters is to decide whether their hosts are to be regarded as intelligent animals or as a lowly type of humanity. For Verne there could be no intermediate stage, no transitional creature capable of 'evolving' into man.

The quest for gold, and its effects upon human nature, are discussed in three of Verne's later narratives. *The Chase of the Golden Meteor* (1908), until recently the only one of his posthumous works to be published in Britain, is aptly summed up in its title. Two amateur astronomers dispute priority in detecting a meteor; at first this is only a matter of prestige, but then spectrum analysis shows that it consists of gold! Another claim is put forward by a scientist who declares that he has brought the meteor to earth by the use of attractive and repulsive rays; here it is clear that Verne was abreast of the latest theories of atomic structure.

There is the usual surprise ending, and much by-play of character. Humour is derived from an elderly servant whose malapropisms form a number of atrocious puns; in spite of his spirited efforts to cope with these, most of them defeated the book's translator! . . .

The Golden Volcano (1906) is no less appropriately named. Bequeathed a claim on the Yukon, two cousins go to the Klondyke to investigate its value. This is in fact a 'Gold Rush' story and for brilliance of description and excitement it vies with the work of Jack London and Robert W. Service, though they knew the region at first hand and Verne only from books. The climb over the Chilkoot Pass and the shooting of the White Horse Rapids are vividly described, as are the hardships and hazards of prospecting; the 'Scout' who leads the expedition to the workings might have been taken from Fenimore Cooper.

Befriended by another pair of cousins—girls this time—but hampered by a gang of unscrupulous rivals, the prospectors work their claim. No sooner does it begin to pay, however, than it is destroyed in a flood, and they have to leave the Yukon for the unexplored regions beyond. The precious metal, they find, is concealed in the depths of a dormant volcano, and their rivals have climbed to the summit and are hurling boulders down on their camp at its foot. One of the cousins is a skilled engineer; can he find no way either of dislodging his adversaries or of inducing the volcano to disgorge its hidden wealth? . . .

The evil effects of the lust for gold form only one of the episodes in *The Survivors of the 'Jonathan'* (1909). This, Verne's most serious work, makes it clear that he had learned much from his experience of municipal politics. Its hero, the Kaw-djer ('Benefactor'), as the natives call him, is an Anarchist—no believer in 'propaganda by deed' and assassination, but an idealist who holds that nothing but evil can come from man's attempts to control his fellow-man. As it transpires that he had voluntarily abandoned rank and wealth, his character may have been suggested by the Austrian Archduke Jean Orth Salvator or by the Russian Prince Kropotkin.

Having fled civilization to dwell in Patagonia, he lives by hunting and fishing; a skilled doctor, he is always ready to befriend the natives and to tend the injured and sick. The wrecking of an emigrant ship on the Chilean coast gives him his longed-for opportunity of setting up a community where there is neither government nor law, and where all are equal and free.

He is quickly disillusioned. One of the emigrants, a Socialist demagogue, gets himself elected as Governor, until his verbose incompetence drives even his docile subjects into revolt. Another is an unscrupulous rascal who under the guise of 'Communism' tyrannizes over the weaklings and extorts their scanty possession and their food.

Appalled, the Kaw-djer watches but cannot bring himself to interfere; though he tirelessly risks infection in tending the sick, he will not lift a finger or say a word to keep anyone from acting as he pleases; that would be to assume the ruling power which he repudiates, to lay down the law that he detests.

At last there comes a crisis and, in response to an appeal from the more level-headed of the community, he becomes its ruler. Firm and benevolent, his wise control makes it flourish, but unforeseeable events put his powers to a very severe test. . . .

The narrative's very effective ending suggests that Verne may have regarded it as his last message to the world, as a solemn leave-taking of human affairs.

There is nothing incongruous in such 'farewells' being made more than once. An aging writer, feeling that this may be the last book he will ever write, may well give it an appropriate ending. Then he may find he has time and strength to write yet another book, and perhaps even a third, each at the time seeming likely to be the last. Surely he may end them appropriately, too, as Verne ended another book with 'those great words, those sublime words, that king of phrases, THE END'.

On 18 April 1914 the Parisians were surprised and delighted to find announced in *Le Matin* 'The Last Strange Journey'. This was not published in book form until 1920, under the rather clumsy title of *L'Etonnante Aventure de la Mission Barsac*, and it recently appeared in Britain, more tersely, as *The Barsac Mission*. (Verne had provisionally called it *A Saharian Town*.)

In spite of its closing words, the story is far from depressing; much of it, indeed, is light in tone, the narrator being a rather flippant French journalist. My impression is that it was partly compiled earlier in Verne's career, but that for some reason he left it unfinished until towards the end of his life.

Its opening words might have been written by Conan Doyle, 'the very accent', Kenneth Allott comments, 'of Watson about to relate another of the cases of Sherlock Holmes.'

> 'Certainly the audacious robbery which the press featured as "The Central Bank Business", and which was front-page news for a fortnight, has not yet been forgotten.'

The first chapter shows that had he wished Verne could have written a thriller comparable with an Edgar Wallace. Much of the book's first part, adventures in the African bush including a visit to a prescient witch-doctor, suggests Rider Haggard; but its second part is pure Jules Vernes and excellent science fiction.

The Barsac Mission is sent into what was then French West Africa to ascertain if its peoples are advanced enough to be given the vote. After certain perplexing incidents its members are kidnapped and imprisoned in Blackland, a mysterious city in the Sahara ruled by a gangster chief.

Accompanying the Mission is an English girl, perhaps the most charming of Verne's heroines; her brother, a British officer, has been convicted of treachery and she seeks to clear his name. Later she learns that her second brother, who has been branded as an accomplice in the bank robbery, is imprisoned by the gangster chief, who cherishes an inveterate hatred for her whole family.

Employed by this villain is a brilliant but unbalanced scientist whose inventions include aircraft (in spite of the development of airplanes Verne had never lost faith in the helicopter), rocket-propelled guided missiles, and weather control. His use of liquid air 'dates' the story, for early in the century this was thought to be the motive-power of the future. Independently of Marconi he has invented wireless telegraphy, and this enables Verne to use his old device, an appeal for help which states the latitude but omits the longitude. . . .

In spite of the claims of both these narratives to convey Verne's farewell to the world, the very last of his *Strange Journeys* is believed to be *The Eternal Adam,* which concludes the posthumous collection *Yesterday and Tomorrow*. As science fiction, as an exciting adventure story, and as an expression of his philosophy, it certainly forms a fitting crown to his life's wcrk.

Its period is the indefinite future and its scene the site of Lost

Atlantis, the tradition of which had always fascinated Verne. Here an aged philosopher discovers a metal tube containing a document in an unknown language, and after much effort he deciphers it. It had been buried, he learns, ages before, by one of the few survivors of a cataclysm which had devastated the whole earth. Though they had found refuge on some land newly arisen above the sea, the mere effort to survive had reduced them almost to the level of animals. Some ancient ruins, the narrator explains, were the vestiges of some primordial civilization older than his, devastated by a volcanic eruption and engulfed in the sea.

The philosopher long remains brooding darkly over this manuscript, which confirms and throws new light on some age-old traditions he already knew. So there had been at least two civilizations before his, that of Atlantis, and that of whose end he had just read —and which was of course our own. As they, and perhaps others before them, had perished, so, no doubt, would his own civilization perish. And even if it were to be succeeded by others yet to come, they, no less undoubtedly, would be equally doomed:

> 'This narrative from beyond the tomb enabled him to imagine the terrible drama forever played throughout the universe, and his heart overflowed with pity. Bleeding from the countless wounds suffered by those who had lived before him, bending beneath the weight of these vain efforts accumulated throughout the infinity of time, he gained, slowly and painfully, an intimate conviction of the eternal recurrence of events.'

XIX
'Onward to Immortality'

NEITHER Verne's literary work nor his duties on the Amiens Municipal Council kept him from having other interests. In 1890, showing unusual enterprise for a cripple of sixty-two, he made a balloon ascent, described in an unpublished trifle, *Twenty-four Minutes in a Balloon.* He was keenly interested in a scheme of M. de la Vaulx for traversing the Mediterranean in a balloon, and he sometimes roused himself to congratulate the energetic people, among them the American journalist Nellie Bly, who had gone around the world in considerably less than eighty days. For the most part, however, he shunned company, and Honorine kept intrusive curiosity-mongers away.

He became an editor of one of Hetzel's magazines, and attended meetings of, and wrote occasional papers for, the Amiens Academy. Though he would not accept mere token association with any society, he was honorary president of the Committee of the Alliance Française and a member of the French Geographical Society. He kept in touch with advances in science, making regular visits to the Reading Room of the Industrial Society of Amiens to consult the latest technical journals.

He was also a member of a local Esperanto Group. The idea of a world language was bound to fascinate him, and he discussed it with his Assyriologist cousin, Colonel Maurice Allotte de la Fuÿe, who did not favour it. Esperantists will regret that he never got further than the preliminary notes of the story he thought of writing on the subject.

All these varied activities he carried out in the face of growing physical and mental distress. His crippling wound necessitated his moving slowly and painfully, leaning heavily on his stick.

Yet this very stick brought a gleam of satisfaction into his sombre life; it was a continual reminder of the happiness that he had given his young readers, for it was a gift from the Boys' Imperial League of Britain. Although Mme de la Fuÿe asserts sentimentally that they meant it to accompany him on his world-wide travels, there is no evidence that they were so naïve; much more probably they knew of his injury, which had been well-publicized, and simply intended it to help him in his everyday walks. Verne was deeply moved by this spontaneous tribute from his young British admirers, whose spokesman explained that as he would understand they were not troubled with overmuch pocket-money so that this gold-mounted stick was the result of a large number of small subscriptions.

Verne's growing depression was not solely due to ill-health and disability. He had suffered many bereavements: it was only in the nature of things that his parents should predecease him, and Hetzel, too, had been his senior by a dozen or so years. But that he should have lost his brother Paul, that was a blow he felt cruelly: 'I would never have thought I should outlive him' was his lament.

Jules Verne's attachment to Paul, and his grief at his loss, are expressed in several of his books, notably *The Sphinx of the Ice-fields*; the heroes of *The Kip Brothers* can face wrongful imprisonment calmly so long as they are together.

Though he knew himself to be read and enjoyed by the younger generation, Verne felt increasingly out of touch with them, born as they were into a world so very different from the one he knew.

That world, too, was disconcerting. In so many ways it was what he had looked forward to so hopefully, yet in so many ways it was not. Here were the most amazing achievements, wonderful inventions and advances in science, the whole earth's being explored until it seemed about to yield up its last secrets. Even the crowning achievements of Hatteras and Captain Nemo, the discovery of the Poles, could only be a question of time.

Access to the newly discovered lands, however, paved the way for their exploitation, and the new inventions and discoveries could so easily be turned to evil ends. During his visit to Germany on the *St Michel III* his sardonic amusements at the antics of its militarists had been swamped by his disquiet at the power of its armaments industry. If he were ever tempted to think that here was a Stahlstadt in real life, events, though he did not live to see them, have justified his forebodings.

Less tragic, not none the less disquieting for one who loved the traditions and culture of his own people, was the spread into Europe of American influence.

Yet however great his forebodings, his faith kept him from the despair which later drove the ageing Wells to write *Mind at the End of its Tether*. If 'science' were to challenge the Almighty, its votaries would meet the fate of Master Zacharius and Robur, and if civilization became altogether materialistic, it would perish like Standard Island and Blackland.

Though a trifling change in natural conditions, as in *The Eternal Adam*, might threaten mankind with destruction, at the worst this would apply only to man's mortal life, and a remnant might still be spared to replenish the earth. And, as in so many of his narratives, a saving few might be spared, preserved, under Providence, by their courage, their integrity, their mutual love and loyalty, and their simple faith.

So he toiled on steadfastly, even when assailed not only by writer's cramp but by the creative artist's besetting fear, that of 'drying up'. When cataract impaired his ability to write, he dictated; he continued his life's work when smitten by partial deafness, when attacks of diabetes warned him that the end could not be far off.

He faced disability and the approach of death with a touch of the mild cynicism with which he had always regarded life. To be deaf in one ear, he commented sardonically, had one consolation: it saved him from hearing half the stupid and wicked things that people say. His diabetes brought on a partial paralysis, and after one crisis he enjoined his wife: 'Next time you had better send for the priest before the doctor, that's all there is to it.'

The priest having heard his confession, Verne declared that he felt regenerated. Knowing that his relatives were grouped round him, he murmured 'So you're all here; now I can go.' Though he failed to recognize his publisher, the younger Hetzel, he made a last gesture of affection towards his wife and son. Then, as his sister said: 'The paralysis spread to the brain and . . . it was no longer our brother or his marvellous intelligence . . . only a body remained.' He had fallen into a coma which lasted till his death at about eight in the morning of Friday, 24 March 1905.

Of William the Silent, it was said that when he died the little children cried in the streets. This would be too much to say of Verne, but certainly with his passing many of his readers felt that they had lost an old and valued friend.

Announced in the press, where it took precedence even of the latest news about the siege of Port Arthur in the Russo-Japanese War, the report of Verne's death brought messages of sympathy to his family from all over the world. His funeral, at the Cemetery de la Madeleine at Amiens, was attended not only by his relatives and friends but by delegates from the learned societies, by a military escort paying tribute to a late Officer of the Legion of Honour, by the local school children, and by many foreign visitors.

One visitor, according to Mlle de la Fuÿe, was a Briton so typical he might have been Phileas Fogg himself. Apparently otherwise ignorant of French, he seemed to have committed one sentence to memory, and he repeated it to each of the chief mourners, '*Courage, courage, dans le dure épreuve qui vous atteint.*'

Subscriptions were soon opened for the erection of monuments to Jules Verne. That of Nantes stands, appropriately enough, at the top of the small Jardin des Plantes; surmounted by a bust of Verne, and with three of his readers shown at its foot, a pedestal bears representations of a train crossing a viaduct, a ship, and a balloon, typifying travel by land, at sea, and in the air.

At Amiens a special theatrical performance was held to raise funds, and an unconventional appeal was made to the public in the local press.[1] Nozier, the author of *Jules Verne et les Fées*, represents the fairies as holding an indignation meeting; their spokesman, the bad godmother Carabosse, declares that Verne is keeping the children from reading fairy-stories and is turning their minds from magic to science. She protests against a monument's being erected to such a man.

But the Fairy Queen points out that Verne is really continuing their own work: the wonders of science are as great as those of magic. How does Cinderella's coach compare with the submarine *Nautilus*, and was not Captain Nemo lured to the ocean depths by the song of the sirens? The fairies, she reminds them, had endowed little Jules at his birth with the gifts of a boundless imagination and tireless energy, and he had used them well. She favours the idea that a monument should be erected to him, and all she asks is that the fairies may appear at its base.

Instead of the fairies, the figures at the base of the statue to Verne at the end of the Jardin Montplaisir, a small park facing his former residence in Amiens, are those of the three children of his old friend,

[1] *Journal d'Amiens*, 15 October 1906.

the Keeper of the city's Museum; two are reading one of his books and the other studying a map.

This statue was raised in 1909, and in 1925 a storm brought down a tree, which in its fall knocked off the heads of three of the figures, those of two of the children and of Verne himself. The damage was left unrepaired for about a year, but at last the heads were replaced.[1]

The most impressive memorial to Verne—like the statue, it is the work of the sculptor Albert Roze—was erected in 1907 over his tomb in the Madeleine cemetery. It shows him, still wrapped in his shroud, as rising from the grave with his arm extended heavenwards: 'ONWARD TO IMMORTALITY AND ETERNAL YOUTH.'

[1] Mme Allotte de la Fuÿe.

XX
'Translations and Tomfooleries'

VERNE was dead, but his work lived on, as indeed it still does. A recent enquiry made by UNESCO shows that he is the most translated of all French authors, and fresh translations of his works are still being made. In Britain an authorized translation of his works, after being serialized in the *Boy's Own Paper*, was published by Messrs Sampson Low Marston and Co., and his more popular stories were produced independently by other firms. The translations vary greatly in quality: most are excellent but some, along with certain adaptations of his work for other media, justify the title, coined by Bernard Shaw, which forms this chapter's heading.

It soon became clear that some of the translators were allowing themselves a certain freedom in adapting his work, many of their alterations being hard to understand. It is easy for British readers to see why the German student Axel, in *Journey to the Centre of the Earth*, should be made half English, but not why Professor Lidenbrock should be renamed Hardwigg! This freedom, too, extended to the titles: in translating Mme de la Fuÿe's biography of Verne, Erik de Maunay found a difficulty in deciding which English version to refer to—some books had four or five different titles, and for others the English title bore no relation to the original at all!

One liberty which was surely justified was the omission of some of the geographical and other technical matter which holds up the story. Not all these omissions were judicious, however, some retaining irrelevant detail while more important material was cut out, and some of the stories being arbitarily curtailed—just to fit the space available in the periodical which first published them.

Far worse than these were actual errors in translation, combined with a clumsiness in diction so great as to suggest that the adaptor was fully conversant neither with Verne's language nor with his own.[1] Some might have been made by a mechanical brain or by a not over-judicious robot, the translator not realizing that when a

[1] Cf. Kingsley Amis's comments in *New Maps of Hell*.

French word looks like an English one it is likely to mean something different, but simply taking the first word that suggested itself. Thus we get, for example, 'deception' for 'disappointment', 'balancing' for 'swinging', and 'apparition' for 'appearance', as well as 'discharging a rifle' and 'stranger' when the context plainly demands 'unloading' and 'foreigner'.

One translator did not know that in France a *temple* is a Protestant church. Another did not realize that, while there are excellent reasons for not speaking of a French lady as *une fille* but always calling her *une jeune fille*, no such rule applies in England, so that there is no need to refer to the heroine painstakingly as a 'young girl' every time she is mentioned, perhaps giving the reader the impression that she is not a young lady but simply a 'kid'.

Some of these errors suggest schoolboy howlers. In *The Castaways of the 'Flag'* an emblem is recognized as British because of 'the red bunting with the yacht in the corner'. Even if his dictionary did not say that the French word *yacht* can mean 'Union Jack', the translator ought to have known what the British Red Ensign looks like. And if he did not, what was he doing translating a sea-story?

Most startling of all, in one version of *Twenty Thousand Leagues* Captain Nemo is made to say that he had constructed the *Nautilus* on an island 'that I could have jumped over if I had liked'. As Macaulay might have commented, 'every schoolboy knows' the colloquial meaning of *faire sauter*, but even if the translator failed to realize that Nemo was declaring that he would have blown up the island if he could, he might have suspected that there was something mildly improbable about his own way of putting it.

Efficient or otherwise, however, the British translators were trying to convey to their readers not what they thought Verne should have written but what he actually wrote. But Edward Roth, the perpetrator—he can hardly be called a translator—of American versions of two of the *Strange Journeys*, had the effrontery to explain that he was 'writing in the style which Verne himself would have used if addressing himself in English to an American audience'.

The result was complimentary neither to Verne nor to his 'American audience'. Roth put in much additional matter, some highly technical—as if there were not quite enough of this in the original—while omitting some of Verne's characteristic touches. He vulgarized the language, not making it 'sexy' but just cheap and slangy. He needlessly altered some of the characters' names and, though this clashed with the illustrations, their appearance. In short he made Verne write as though he were not Jules Verne but Edward Roth.

Had his versions, dating from 1874, been allowed to sink into the oblivion they deserve, there would be no need to mention them here. Unfortunately, however, they have recently been given a new lease of life as paperbacks; and, with an effrontery even greater than that of Roth himself, the American publishers announce them as 'the most faithful and readable version'. It is a pity that a reputable British firm has associated itself with these atrocities, but surely they would not have done so had they known the facts.

Again to adapt Macaulay, Roth, 'ill as he has performed his task, has at least this claim to our gratitude' that he has enabled us to see some of the original illustrations once again. Verne was very fortunate in his illustrators[1] who admirably conveyed the spirit of his work. As was to be expected, some of the recent editions very effectively use all the resources of colour printing, but lovers of Verne will regret the delightful black-and-white drawings that appeared in the early editions of *Captain Hatteras* and *Journey to the Centre of the Earth.*

Not that all those early illustrations were happy. The immense gun in *The Begum's Fortune* appears merely as an enlarged version of a contemporary cannon, with the result that its controls tower high above its inventor's head, and are so large that only a giant could handle them!

Like d'Ennery, Roth had been born too soon and missed his vocation. Had he lived in recent times and worked in Hollywod, he could have adapted the *Strange Journeys* to his heart's content, producing results which in his opinion Verne would have produced had Verne been a film producer.

The film industry, which, not content with taking appalling liberties with biography, history, legend, and the masterpieces of literature, has not scrupled to tamper with Holy Writ, could not be expected to treat Verne and more respectfully. Too often it has used his narratives only as a basis for its own plots, distorting incident and character out of all recognition. Nor has it hesitated to vulgarize an author remarkable for his austerity.

[1] See Edmondo Marcucci, *Les Illustrations des 'Voyages Extraordinaires' de Jules Verne.*

Twenty Thousand Leagues, magnificent film though it would have made if followed faithfully, has been one of the greatest sufferers. The screen version was so good, where it did keep to the book, that its vulgarities were all the more jarring. The burial in the sea-floor, the *Nautilus* gliding through the ocean depths like some prehistoric monster, were magnificent. It is in such work that the cinema excels.

The film's greatest fault lay in its perversion of Ned Land's character. Verne had shown him as one of nature's gentlemen, grave, taciturn, and cultured, and spending his leisure moments reading: his 'recital of his adventures in the polar seas', said Aronnax, 'took the form of an epic poem . . . a Canadian Homer singing the Iliad of the North.'

Hollywood no doubt found such a character incredible, but they might at least have made him decent. Instead they depicted him as a dissolute ruffian, staggering about with a disreputable-looking female on each arm, and wantonly destroying valuable biological specimens to drink the alcohol in which they were preserved; this, presumably, was meant for humour.

Michael Strogoff was treated more seriously, but when it came to dealing with the 'blinding' scene, its producers were, not surprisingly, unable to accept Verne's explanation. One version suggested that the executioner had been bribed to spare his victim, incredible though the circumstances made this. Another invoked a miracle, a 'vision' appearing on the screen at a critical moment to convey this to the audience.

To judge by a radio excerpt from *Five Weeks in a Balloon*, the film was the most appalling travesty of Verne's work. On the other hand, in spite of the liberties they took with the original, the cinema versions of *The Mysterious Island* and *Mathias Sandorf* were exciting and amusing.

So was the film of *Journey to the Centre of the Earth*, though this had little in common with the narrative, except the general idea that anyone who descends the crater of an extinct volcano may expect to find something unexpected at its foot. It introduced a murderous rival to the speleological expedition—which for box-office purposes had to be burdened with a heroine—and got much cheap humour out of the Icelandic guide, whom Verne had made so estimable. To be fair, however, it did quote one sentence from the book, though out of its context; and perhaps by way of making amends it interpolated episodes from other Verne books: the 'magnetic storm', most improbably, from *Sphinx of the Ice-fields*, and the visit to lost Atlantis from *Twenty Thousand Leagues*.

The most spectacular Verne film, *Around the World in Eighty Days*, was marred by the usual liberties: a balloon trip had to be inserted, for example, simply because the author was associated with aerial travel. Its worst fault was its touches of crass vulgarity, and though it followed the book only in general outline it was certainly worth seeing. If it had kept more faithful to the original it would have been better still.

The nadir of absurdity was reached in the film entitled *Master of the World*, whose plot owed something to the two Robur stories; it is tempting to believe that H. G. Wells's *Time Machine* had somehow got dragged into the studios. An aircraft of the future is shown as dropping bombs of a present-day type—and their target is a three-masted line-of-battle sailing-ship. When she soars above London, local colour and verisimilitude is given by the brief appearance on the screen of *Old* London Bridge—the house-crowded bridge which was demolished about 1832—followed by that of the modern Houses of Parliament! Then the aircraft is shown bombing the sailing-ships of the Royal Navy in London Pool.

In Search of the Castaways was based on *The Children of Captain Grant*: excellent film though it was, and refreshingly free from vulgarity, it introduced some needless alterations. One, however, is understandable: in the original and in d'Ennery's stage version, the young heroine is respectively shown as likely to marry the ship's captain and Lord Glenarvan, men decidedly older than herself. As such an idea would be unacceptable to modern teenagers, his Lordship had to be given a son of about her own age, enabling the film to end with the inevitable suggestion of wedding-bells.

Films are so ruinously expensive to produce that some alterations are justifiable, such as the judicious introduction of a heroine in a story devoid of feminine interest. *For the Flag* would not be ruined if the nurse-technician Simon Hart were to become Simone! The heroic naval officer who figures in the narrative could be spectacularly rescued; and after being married at sea by the ship's chaplain, the happy pair could sail, while the flotilla's guns thunder a salute, into the conventional polychromatic sunset.

If any film producer dare attempt so unprecedented an innovation, some of Verne's finest works could be followed without alteration: *Black Diamonds, North against South*, and *A Family Without a Name. The Green Ray* would form a light romance, and if horror were needed there is *Carpathian Castle.*

Such possibilities, however, are hypothetical, and meantime there is something in the screen industry's favour. It has vulgarized Jules Verne, maltreated his characters, distorted his work out of all reason, and even—in *Five Weeks in a Balloon*—made him seem absurd. But it has not made him dull.

That achievement was reserved, I regret to state, for our own B.B.C. Of its version of *Twenty Thousand Leagues,* produced for juvenile auditors, all that need be said is that any boy who heard it must have felt that, considered as a writer of science fiction, Jules Verne had been singularly overrated.

XXI
Verne in Literature

IT WOULD take one of Verne's compatriots to judge his position among the literary figures of France. One critic has compared him with Corneille, and another, describing his style as typically Breton, with such authors as Chateaubriand and Renan.[1] It may well be that he achieved his ambition and became the Dumas of science fiction, aiming not at classical correctness but at 'lived and living scenes'. But though like Dumas he wrote historical stories these were never so popular as those with a scientific basis.

Among Verne's faults was a tendency to slur over his endings, as though his mind were already more concerned with his next book. Occasionally, too, he skipped an episode that seemed to call for full treatment. Phileas Fogg sets out to rescue Passepartout, taken prisoner by the Indians; and after a time he brings him back in triumph—and that is all. How the rescue was accomplished we are not told.

Verne also had some rather curious mannerisms, sometimes copied by his translators and sometimes omitted. Instead of saying, for example, 'The captain did so-and-so', he has a trick of putting it 'As for the captain, he did so-and-so', though nothing is gained by this oblique construction.

A few books have no titles for the chapters; for many the titles are short but explicit. But for some the titles are an inordinate length, extending to two or three lines perhaps, and begin in the rather archaic style 'In which . . .' so-and-so happens. I get the impression that Verne used this needless verbiage when he was not really gripped by his story, when 'words would not come' to him—and I find it significant that this applies to his brilliant idea, so disappointingly worked out, *The Clipper of the Clouds.*

Verne's work is so obviously didactic that he might be regarded less as a story-teller than as a geographer and a popularizer of science,

[1] C. Lemire.

using the fictional form simply because that was his only way in conveying information to the public.

It was not that he regarded the factual detail in his narrative as the pill in a spoonful of jam; to his mind the pill was part of the jam. So great was his interest in geography and general science that he may well have taken it for granted that his readers shared it.

To some extent they may actually have done so. Nowadays most of us have a general idea of conditions in different parts of the world, and in the broad outlines of scientific theory; or if not we can very easily find out.

A century ago such knowledge was far less widespread: popular education was almost in its infancy, readable popularizations were few, and there was no cinema or television to display exotic scenery. At the same time the achievements of explorers and scientists alike were arousing widespread interest in newly investigated regions of the earth and regions of thought.

Though Verne always had his youthful readers in mind, he seldom wrote expressly for them. The widespread impression that he did—in the public libraries his works are more likely to be found in the juvenile than the adult collections, and one reviewer rebuked me mildly for raising in my introduction to the Verne story issues 'surely remote to the average young reader'—may be largely due to his works having first appeared in Britain serialized in the *Boy's Own Paper*. Yet is it not unreasonable: young readers will accept uncritically statements which thoughtful adults would question.

A boy, lost in the excitement of the story, will fail to reflect that if an outlaw-gang take a prisoner they are hardly likely to supply him with unlimited writing-material, and still less likely to leave his writings unread; nor that in such circumstances the captive would hardly be so naïve as to confide to paper his inmost thoughts, including his schemes for sending out an appeal for help!

Nor is a young reader likely to be as sceptical as an adult when Verne yields to one of his weaknesses, a shameless use of coincidence. A speleologist, lost and panic-stricken in the bowels of the earth, drops exhausted at the one point where his voice will reach his comrades along a natural whispering-gallery; a boat-load of castaways on the verge of starvation drifts through the uncharted polar wastes within sight of a rescue expedition. Though he may suppress his doubts in the excitement of the narrative, such incidents startle an adult, but the boy takes them in his stride.

Akin to this is Verne's predilection for 'last moment' rescues—how many of his characters are saved just as all help seems lost? He uses the same technique even when no question of peril is involved, as when Captain Nemo is able to 'pin-point' the South Pole by shooting the sun only as it is about to sink below the horizon for the long polar night.

This may be deliberate. A religious man, Verne may have regarded chance occurrences as providential[1] and have felt fully justified in making use of them. The words he puts in the mouth of Captain Len Guy, 'God is guiding us', might equally have been spoken by his other heroes. Whether this trust in Providence arose from his first-hand experience it is not for me to say, but so far-reaching were the results of his submitting his manuscript to Hetzel that he might be pardoned for feeling that his wife had been providentially guided in sending him to that publisher's door. Readers of his own generation, more religious-minded than ourselves, may have found it easier to accept such guidance than we are; and it is possible that but for our scepticism we might find evidence for it even in our own lives.

Young readers, accustomed to the melodrama of sound-films, radio, and television, are less likely than adults to be amused or repelled when a Verne character, 'bleeding sawdust' as Kenneth Allott epigramatically puts it, waxes magniloquent, like Captain Nemo addressing the setting sun:

> '*Adieu*, thou sun; Disappear, thou radiant orb! Depart to thy rest beneath this open sea, and let a night six months long cast its shadow over my new domain!"

Not all Verne's characters are so wooden as has been made out: in *A Family Without a Name*, for example, they are clearly and sympathetically drawn, and even in his science fiction and adventure stories they may develop in response to life. The growing mental instability of Captain Hatteras is depicted as clearly as his mate's gradual descent from determination to irresolution and thence to open mutiny; Hatteras and his American rival are transformed from bitter enmity into frank comradeship; Captain Nemo's unavail-

[1] M. Moré, 'Hazard et Providence chez Jules Verne', in *Critique*, May 1962.

ing remorse reduces him from a Byronic hero into a fugitive from his own conscience.

On the whole, however, Verne's characterization tends to be 'in black and white', another feature which appeals less to adults than to young readers, who like to know where they are. His heroes are stalwart and idealistic, resourceful, self-sacrificing, regardless of hardship and peril while pursuing worth-while ends, the sort of people that most of us would like to be. Similarly, his villains are satisfyingly bad, and nobody is likely to shed any tears over them when they meet their doom.

Yet—and this helped to endear his books to parents—his villains are 'nicely' bad. Except in the posthumous *Barsac Mission,* written when Verne—or his editor—was influenced by the tendencies of the age, they may threaten a woman with death, but not with 'a fate worse than death'.

Even in that book, however, Verne shows a typical reticence. Its villain's inveterate and baseless hatred for the noble family he had entered into is explained, rather unconvincingly, as due to his being not the son, but only the stepson, of its head. A modern author would much more plausibly have made him the nobleman's illegitimate son, enraged at having no claim on his father's rank and wealth.

Verne protested against the idea that women appeared but little in his work. 'Whenever they are necessary,' he declared, 'they will be found.' True, and wherever they are not necessary, as in most of his science fiction, they are left out. His heroines, he claimed, were 'adorable girls'; and his heroes, too, are clean-living. He always sought to avoid anything which could not be placed without hesitation in the hands of youth, anything which a boy—of Victorian times, of course—'would not like to see in his sister's hands'.

Whatever the cynic may say, there is something to be said for this attitude. The adventure-lover or science fiction addict may find a Verne story held up for passages of more or less relevant technical detail, but not by quite irrelevant descriptions of courtship, or, worse still, of some sordid adultery or seduction. (And those who like that sort of thing will hardly enjoy having to wade through pages of adventure or science fiction to find it.)

There was no place in Verne's work for passionate or sensual love, desire, or jealousy, or eternal triangle nonsense, but that from his point of view was an advantage. 'Maybe the widespread diffusion of my works', he said, 'is chiefly due to my doing what I have always set out to do, not to publish a page or a phrase which could not be read by the young people whom I write for and love.'[1]

In Verne characterization is always subsidiary to the plot, usually the record of some worthwhile achievement. Freed from excessive technical matter, his narratives are full of exciting action, enlivened by humour and with unexpected turns leading up to his favourite literary device, in which he forestalled O. Henry, the Vernian surprise ending. Very seldom throughout his work does he repeat an incident, and only once, I think, does he repeat it twice, in the geographical location with the missing longitude (and only his most inveterate readers would notice the repetition). For the most part, though he recurs time and again to his favourite scenes, the jungle, the ice-fields, or the desert island, he always finds something new to say about them, some unexpected episode of which they form the background.

Subordinate to plot as they are, however, his characters are memorable. Dr Fergusson and his companions; Hatteras and Dr Clawbonny; Lidenbrock and his nephew and Hans the guide; the three pioneer astronauts; Captain Nemo and Aronnax; Phileas Fogg and Passepartout; Michael Strogoff—they may be wildly improbable, but they do stick in the memory, and most of them are great fun.

It was in other fields for the imagination that Verne excelled. Scenes never beheld by man become almost visible in his pages, the most fantastic creatures seem alive. The African jungle as seen from the air; the fantastic shapes, like the architecture of some dreamland city, of the icebergs; the cavities deep in the heart of the rocks and the sunless ocean into which they lead; the starry sky, the distant earth, and the lunar surface as viewed from the hurtling space-capsule; the coral forests that clothe the sea-floor and the ruins of lost Atlantis—all these are described with vivid realism. And on that sea-floor, along the approaches to that lost city, live creatures unknown to the land-dwellers.

> 'Millions of luminous points gleamed in the midst of the darkness. They were the eyes of gigantic creatures crouched in their lairs; of giant lobsters, erect like halberdiers and waving their

[1] C. Lemire.

> claws with a metallic clicking; of titanic crabs, pointed like a gun on its carriage; and of frightful squids, interweaving their tentacles like a living nest of serpents.'

He can convey, too, the emotive nature of those scenes, as in Dr Clawbonny's musings as his vessel coasts the Greenland wastes:

> 'The strange history of this region passed through the Doctor's mind as he leaned on the rail and followed with his eyes the long wake left by the brig. Thoughts of its daring navigators crowded into his memory, and he fancied he could perceive, below the frozen crests of the icebergs, the pale ghosts of those who would return no more.'

XXII
Founder of Science Fiction

JULES VERNE did not actually 'create' science fiction, which is the modern development of an art-form older than written literature, the wonder story. This, like his own works, might have a realistic basis: ingenious attempts have been made, for example, to discover the facts behind the travels of Odysseus, the Argonauts, and Sindbad the Sailor. Even the space-travel theme dates back to the second century A.D., though Lucian's *True History* was intended merely as a skit on travellers' tall stories; Kepler's *Somnium* had this in common with modern science fiction, that it was based on up-to-date technical information.

Most of these early stories fall into two groups. If they are not pure romancing, written only to entertain, like Lucian's, they have an ulterior motive: satire, like Dean Swift's *Gulliver*,[1] or utopianization, like Bacon's *New Atlantis*. In spite of its title, Poe's *The Balloon Hoax* (1844) is probably the earliest example of 'straight' science fiction; it describes plausibly, and with reassuring technical detail, the flight of a dirigible balloon across the Atlantic.

In this, as in his *Hans Pfall* story, Poe made it clear that he was only romancing, and that he had completely failed to foresee the possibilities of science fiction. Verne was the first to realize them clearly, take them seriously, and exploit them systematically. It is in this sense that he can be regarded as the founder of science fiction.

Sheer romancing figures little in his work, and satire and utopianization play only a minor part in it. His great aim was to impart information through the medium of an exciting story, and to this end he described his heroes' achievements with almost a documentary precision; he always sought to be able to give 'chapter and verse' for the conditions they encounter and the methods they use.

Here he contrasts sharply with H. G. Wells, of whom it might be

[1] Not usually regarded as science fiction, but his Book III, the 'Voyage to Laputa', certainly is, including the usual technical explanation complete with illustrative diagram.

said that he would have founded science fiction had not Verne forestalled him. Wells gave his imagination much freer range and was not so scrupulous about the factual basis. Both fully realized the difference, and would never have regarded themselves as the French-English equivalents of one another. Verne seems to have felt that Wells was an incompetent interloper, making an unfair use of sheer impossibilities. Of Wells's *First Men in the Moon* he is quoted in *T.P.'s Weekly* as saying:

> 'I make use of physics. He invents. I go to the moon in a cannon-ball, discharged from a cannon. Here there is no invention. He goes to Mars in an airship, which he constructs of a metal which does away with the law of gravitation. That's all very well, but show me this metal. Let him produce it.'

In the Introduction to his *Collected Scientific Romances* Wells, on the other hand, pays tribute to Verne but stresses their differences.

> 'These tales have been compared with the work of Jules Verne, and there was a disposition on the part of literary journalists at one time to call me the English Jules Verne. As a matter of fact there is no literary resemblance whatever between the anticipatory inventions of the great Frenchman and these fantasies. His work dealt almost always with actual possibilities of invention and discovery and he made some remarkable forecasts. The interest he invoked was a practical one; he wrote and believed and told that this thing or that could be done, which was not at that time done. He helped his reader to imagine it done and to realize what fun, excitement or mischief might ensue. Many of his inventions have "come true". But these stories of mine collected here do not pretend to deal with possible things; they are exercises of the imagination in a quite different field.'

In his treatment of technical detail Wells is much less documentary than Verne, seeking to get his effects not by matter-of-fact description but by imaginative boldness. As Macaulay said of Dante and Milton, 'we can compare the exact details of the one with the dim intimations of the other'.

One the other hand, when it comes to real flights of the imagination, it is Verne who is vague and Wells who goes into detail. When Verne's super-speleologists meet a prehistoric giant, their one desire, reasonably enough, is to get away from him. When Wells's heroes are able to study unearthly creatures, they describe them graphically and at some length.

The contrast between the two authors is even more strikingly shown in the ideas which they were the first to give to science fiction.[1] These make it obvious that they were thinking on different mental 'wave-lengths'.

Those of Verne include journeys into the bowels of the earth, into the depths of the sea, and into outer space; aircraft and submarines of extraordinary efficiency, including the triphibious *Épouvantable*; such weapons as poison-gas, incendiary bombs, and rocket-propelled guided missiles, one having in small compass the destructive force of a block-buster; the survival into modern times of prehistoric animals; amazing feats of engineering, including the construction of an artificial island; weather control; the use of attractive and repulsive rays; and the devastation of the whole earth. Though not the first to imagine the possibility of an artificial satellite, he popularized the idea; and though he did not foresee the atomic bomb as such, he had an inkling of something almost as dreadful.[2]

Even some of his minor ideas, which he put forward facetiously, have been shown by his successors as amenable to serious treatment. Dr Ox, influencing a community's thoughts, is suggestive of Big Brother in fiction and Dr Goebbels in real life. Gil Braltar leading the apes of 'the Rock' to attack its garrison has been excelled in science fiction by experts training a variety of animals to wage super-scientific warfare. More seriously, the failure of the time-keepers of Master Zacharius is the first example of what in some modern science fiction stories has been called the 'death of metal'.

Wells's contributions to science fiction include time travel: the 'fourth dimension', the conversion of animals, by vivisection, into humanoid beings; human invisibility; invasion from outer space; giantism in plant, animal, and man; intelligent insects; blood-sucking plants; aerial warfare; and such weapons as the heat ray, gases whose

[1] Naturally they had no monopoly of these ideas, some of which were probably rediscovered, quite independently, by later authors.

[2] *For the Flag* has been regarded as a forecast of the atomic bomb, but the story makes it clear that what Verne had in mind was a 'conventional' weapon, though of unprecedented force. (It will be seen that I have not mentioned the ideas which Verne is said to have derived from Robida.)

touch brings death, tanks, anti-tank flame-throwers, tank-trapping slime-pits, and the atomic bomb.

The contrast is still clearer when they discuss similar themes. The *Nautilus* is attacked by gigantic squids; Wells's prototype bathyscaph, by humanoid fish. Verne's future world is ruled by an arbitrary but benevolent journalist, that of Wells by a grim financial oligarchy overthrown by a ruthless dictator.

So many of these writers' inventions have 'come true' that it is not surprising that they have both been regarded, half seriously and half facetiously, as 'prophets'. One of the most remarkable of these forecasts was made not by the matter-of-fact but by the imaginative writer.

If while touring Italy Verne studied the works of Leonardo da Vinci, he must have seen his sketches of an armoured war-chariot; and he can hardly have helped noticing a serio-comic illustration in the *Musée des Familles* depicting motorized caravans and self-propelled cannon crossing a battlefield strewn with mangled corpses. Yet unless Behemoth, the mechanized elephant of *The Steam House*, is regarded as something of the sort, it was not Verne but Wells who first foresaw the tanks (in his short story *The Land Ironclads*, 1903).

The probability is that the macabre 'humour' of that illustration in the *Musée* was lost on Verne; seeing only the horror, he declined to introduce anything of the sort into a narrative. Wells equally realized the potential dreadfulness of the tanks, but minimized it: the shooting of the automatic rifles in his Land Ironclads is so accurate that their adversaries are either killed outright or forced into surrender.

That Verne's ideas should seem so matter-of-fact compared with those of later science fiction authors is because he had not less imagination than they, but more. He did not need to turn to other worlds to find strange surroundings or strange creatures; there were plenty of both on our own earth.

Why should he imagine what are now called BEMs—'Bug-eyed monsters'—on some distant planet when the world is so full of them? What fantastic creature from 'space opera' is as strange as an insect seen through a lens or the inhabitants of the ocean depths? What writer, if he had not known that such things exist as, for example, a monstrous beast which uses its nose as a hand, would ever have dreamed of them?—or have thought it possible that small relations of the fierce tiger and the predatory wolf would make delightful household pets?

Can any other-worldly landscapes be imagined more outlandish than some of the regions of earth? Who, if he had not read descriptions of them, could have visualized the ice-fields, the deserts, the jungle, the Bad Lands of Dakota? There was plenty of scope for Verne's imagination here on earth.

Even less happy than their attempts to describe extra-terrestrial creatures or landscapes have been the efforts of the science fiction writers to imagine non-human cultures. Such civilizations, however different they are made to seem from ours, have a disconcerting trick of suddenly revealing that they are uncommonly like our own.

Verne did not have to leave earth to find strange cultures, or even to range so widely as the Far East or the distant West. Just across the Rhine was the queerest mixture of pedantry and militarism. Just across the Atlantic lived business-men of great enterprise, engineers of matchless technical efficiency, yet with a preposterous froth of 'Barnums', and with the strangest habits of clotting into fantastic societies and settling their quarrels not by civilized duels but by a merciless fight to the death. (' "What demons you are!" cried Michel Ardan. "Yes, we are!" J. T. Maston replied modestly.')

Strangest of all, just across the Channel were a people who seemed to do everything the wrong way round, to whom the 'right' side of a street was the left side, who with a vestigial grammar and a fantastic spelling had produced a great literature, who with an equally fantastic system of weights and measures were carrying on a flourishing industry and commerce, and whose Christianity, though incredibly fragmented, had a most salutary effect upon the national character.

Whether it was a question of creatures, landscapes, or cultures, Verne would hardly have been surprised to find that the most imaginative writers of space opera would be outdistanced by the geographer. He was too religious-minded to suppose that men could ever be more creative than the Creator!

Apart from the method and the themes he gave science fiction, he had also endowed it with humour, idealism, and vivid, if rather improbable, characterization. In other hands, though certainly not in those of Wells, it might have been repulsively dull.

One other service Verne performed for science fiction: he made it austere. There is neither vulgarity nor undue violence in his writings, and though the lack of a love-interest may be regarded as a merit or otherwise, it is certainly well that there should be a complete absence of lust.

Wells, considered as a writer of science fiction, was equally austere, as were almost all of its other pioneers, notably Hugo Gernsback—who founded the first successful magazine of what he once thought of calling 'scientifiction'—and the other editors of such early magazines.

Nor has this tradition been completely lost. Though, as might have been expected, science fiction has suffered from the present disease of literature, a bewildering vagueness of style, and the intrusion of morbid themes of sex and violence even where the story does not require them, this applies to only a minority of its authors. Some of them, moreover, give the impression of having yielded to such weaknesses reluctantly, with the idea of appealing to some fancied public demand, so obviously are they out of place.

So, we may hope, sex and violence will clearly become so completely needless in such literature that they will be discarded. Then science fiction will return, with a sigh of relief, to the austerity bestowed upon it by Jules Verne.

Then, too, we may hope, it will shake off another of its modern aberrations, some stories being so verbosely allusive that readers may find it hard to make head or tail of them. Verne, though he might clog his story with technical detail, was almost always clear, and so was Wells, as were many of the other pioneers.

Had science fiction been founded by Poe, it would have had a morbid twist and abounded in silly mystifications and hoaxes and other forms of facetiousness. Had it been founded by Wells, it would have been less documentary and made a wider use of the imagination, taking more liberties with ascertained fact. Had it been founded by some—some only—of the modern writers, it would have been more turgid and involved and far less austere.

Wells and his successors have of course developed it in their own characteristic ways, and in its future developments it will no doubt evolve more diversely still. But whatever it may become, we may be certain of one thing, that it will never cease to display the influence of its founder Jules Verne.

XXIII
Verne and the Modern World

H. G. WELLS said that many of Verne's forecasts have 'come true'—and so, for that matter, have many of his own; sometimes spoken of as a Wellsian world, this is a Vernian world also. Deep caverns, if not an actual volcanic crater, have been explored, and subterranean lakes and rivers, if not a subterranean ocean, have been reached. Huge submarines, with amenities as remarkable as those of Captain Nemo, have traversed the ocean depths and reached not indeed the South Pole but the North. Helicopters and other 'aeronefs' have superseded the 'aerostat', the dirigible balloon. A creature far more ancient than Verne's prehistoric monsters, the coelacanth, has survived into modern times; weapons more horrible than he imagined have produced more devastating effects than he foresaw. True, artificial islands like self-propelled 'Mulberry Harbours' have not yet cruised across the Pacific, nor has weather control been achieved, but neither of these achievements would surprise us overmuch.

Verne—and Wells—may have done far more than to foretell such developments; they may actually have helped to bring them about. At the beginning of the century the 'practical men' were pooh-poohing the idea of 'flying-machines' just as much more recently they were pooh-poohing the idea of space travel, lectures on the latter subject often arousing two seemingly-irrefutable objections: 'What's the use of it?' and 'If space travel were possible, would anyone be courageous enough to go?'

None of Verne's young readers would have found it difficult to answer these questions; far from doubting that flight and space travel were possible, they were certain that these would be achieved. Their minds filled with such nonsense, as their elders called it, these pioneer science fiction addicts did not discard it as they reached maturity. So there arose a generation ready to welcome flight and space travel as soon as they appeared, and among these enthusiasts were engineers willing to experiment with gliders and rockets and industrialists willing to produce them, so that at last the gliders became airplanes and the rockets carried space-capsules beyond the air.

Nor was there any lack of volunteers willing to risk their lives manning them, to become the forerunners in real life of Robur and Michel Ardan. Indeed there were far more than were needed, a wealth of splendid human material from whom were chosen only those able to pass exacting tests. The first of all space-travellers, the Russian cosmonaut Yuri Gagarin, has declared how much he owed to his reading of Jules Verne.

So the one question raised by the doubters was answered. And as for the other, why anyone should wish to 'conquer space'? Whatever may be said about the military advantages or economic possibilities of such projects, surely the real unspoken answer is that given by Mallory when asked why he wished to climb Mount Everest: 'Because it's there!'

Submarine development similarly owes much to Verne, whose forecasted *Nautilus* was so far ahead of his time that it seemed as fantastic as the *Albatross* or the manned space-capsule fired at the moon. 'There's no proof that we shall ever be able to go travelling about under the seas like that,' commented a friendly fisherman, speaking from his long experience of the sea. 'M'sieu Verne is just spinning us tall stories.' That probably summed up the general opinion, but, simply by describing a perfected submarine, the narrative helped to bring it into being.

The debt which submarine development owes to Verne is well expressed by the names of the vessels which made two of the most ambitious undersea voyages of modern times. In 1931 Sir George Hubert Wilkins, working on the plausible but incorrect assumption that the lower surface of the ice-floes is level—it is in fact as irregular as their upper surface—tried to reach the North Pole by fitting runners on his vessel's deck and attempting to skid along beneath the ice; though he failed, his remarkable feat of Arctic exploration added much to geographical science. In 1958, commanded by Captain Anderson of the United States Navy, the first atomic-powered submarine actually 'pierced' the Pole by cruising beneath the icefields. It seemed not merely appropriate but almost inevitable that both vessels should be called *Nautilus*. Had not Verne foreseen their achievements, not indeed in detail but in spirit? What else could these vessels have possibly been called?

Certainly Verne would have been delighted had he known that, like the balloon *Victoria*, the two modern *Nautili* would have been used not in warfare but in exploration. This theme is developed by the Russian writer, Cyrille Andreev, in his introduction to the translation of the *Complete Works of Jules Verne* published in the Soviet Union.

'Early submarines', he reminds us, 'were exclusively used for military purposes. Bourgeois society could have imagined no other use for them . . . *Twenty Thousand Leagues*', he continues, 'owes its charm to Captain Nemo . . . under whose command the *Nautilus* from a weapon of destruction becomes a floating laboratory.'

It was, we are assured, Verne's love for freedom and hatred of imperialism and capitalism that preserved him from being one of the bourgeoisie. We may infer, too, that Captain Nemo's wanton crippling of an American frigate does not count, any more than does his destruction of two British warships, involving the wholesale slaughter of their crews; these vessels, after all, belonged to the 'capitalist-imperialist' powers.

Speleology, the scientific investigation of caverns, is an important branch of geology, and a subject with which even the most carefree caver does well to have a nodding acquaintance. The science and sport of cave-exploration alike owe much to Verne. Norman Casteret, whose *Ten Years under the Earth* is a speleological classic, said that it was reading *Journey to the Centre* which first turned his thoughts underground.

It is impossible to estimate how far Verne's forecasts have influenced invention and stimulated scientists or explorers to embark on their chosen careers. Byrd, Beebe, Yuri Gagarin, Norman Casteret, Marconi, and Santos Dumont, by no means exhaust the list of those who were inspired by his *Strange Journeys*. In lighter vein, Dr Hale of Palomar Observatory was fond of quoting a sentence from *Round the Moon*: 'A frightful cry was heard, and the unfortunate man disappeared into the telescope.'

Literature owes more to Jules Verne than his success in founding its new branch, science fiction. Writers of adventure stories, for adults as well as for young people, learned from him to introduce into their narratives the contemporary achievements of science or engineering, though without falling into his own mistake of going into too much detail. Thus developed what might be called 'technical fiction', the type of literature in which Nevil Shute excelled.

Verne's adventure stories have now acquired a further use, though for this their unabridged form, with all its geographical detail, would be essential. The mere effluxion of time has converted them into historical fiction, with the additional advantage that they were written by a contemporary writer. Anyone wishing to learn the conditions that prevailed in distant lands during the nineteenth century would do well to consult whichever of the *Strange Journeys* dealt with those regions. *Five Weeks in a Balloon*, for example, might well become recommended reading in the emergent native states of Africa, showing their peoples what they might still have been were it not for the white man.

Though they are now historical, instead of contemporary, fiction and though much of their technical background, though based on the accepted beliefs of the time, has now been superseded, Verne's stories have by no means lost either their value or their appeal. Though the feat it describes is now known to be impossible, *Journey to the Centre of the Earth* can still interest a geologist and still induce young readers to study his science. *Round the Moon* conveys as much as ever the fascination of outer space; *Twenty Thousand Leagues*, that of the uncharted ocean deeps. Verne's characters are still attractive, inspiring the reader even while they amuse him, making him realize that better than the desire for wealth or social status, perhaps more compelling even than the mating instinct, is 'the call of the wild', that longing for adventure in the real world or in the world of thought which leads some to become explorers and others to devote themselves to scientific research.

XXIV
Personal Life and Philosophy

APART from his early struggles, his occasional cruises in his yacht, and the heroism with which he faced his disability, there is little to say about Jules Verne's personal life. As he replied[1] when Professor Mario Turiello of Naples said what a pleasure it would give the public if he wrote an account of his life and travels:

> 'I do not agree, my friend, and I've never thought of doing it. An account of my travels would have very little interest for my readers, and the story of my life would have no more. A writer interests his public only as a writer.'

He was devoted to his work and sedulous in performing his duties as a municipal councillor. Apart from his interest in the theatre he had little time for recreation, and his amusements were intellectual, an interest in cryptograms and other verbal problems and an addiction to atrocious puns. He did not make friends easily and had little use for social amenities, discouraging casual visitors and refusing to indulge in time-wasting sidelines. He could never suffer fools gladly, and his character resembled that of a minor character in *Mrs Branican*:

> 'This personage was a veritable bear, not one of the American grizzlies with claws and fur but one of those human bears who seek above all to live outside of any social relation.'

He once owned a Newfoundland dog called 'Follet',[2] a name which might be translated 'playful', 'goblin', or 'silky haired'—it was characteristic that Verne should pun even on a pet's name, and had he been alive today he might have carried the pun further by speaking of this as a 'shaggy dog story'. Many dogs figure in his

[1] In a letter quoted by Lemire.
[2] G. H. Waltz.

narratives, from Captain Hatteras's faithful Duk (? Dick or Duke) to Captain Pip's 'twin soul . . . a dirty yellow cur', Mizzen, in *The Thompson Travel Agency.* The most talented is Dingo, the mongrel in *The Boy Captain,* which can recognize its former master's initials!

In marked contrast to Wells, who was a 'cat man', Verne seems to have had a bias against cats. In *The Village in the Treetops* he mentions them as a by-word for spitefulness; and when, in *From the Earth to the Moon,* a cat forestalls the Russian dog Laika in paving the way for human space-travel, it shows its appreciation of the privilege by eating its fellow-traveller, the first martyr to astronautical science, J. T. Maston's pet squirrel!

Verne's family life seems to have been quite happy. That, apart from his ambitions, he wanted to leave his father's home is understandable, for Pierre Verne was rather a formidable person with a mania for punctuality. None the less, Jules never lost his affection and respect for him, and he was devoted to his mother and on the best of terms with his brother Paul.

Though his wife Honorine may have found some of his vagaries a little trying, their marriage was successful, as he showed by paying her the delicate compliment of making several of his heroes marry widows even when the plot does not necessitate this. There is no suggestion that he was ever unfaithful to her: apart from his Church's teaching, which he took very seriously, he may have felt, even if he ever considered burdening himself with such an encumbrance, that to keep a mistress would involve an appalling waste of time.

He seems to have been very little troubled by sex. He was content with one son, and may indeed have had him 'on principle', as an heir, to ensure the family name, and possibly to demonstrate his own virility. Certainly sex does not figure greatly in his stories; not only many of his heroes but even some of his villains, like the pirates in *For the Flag,* seem to be content with no female companionship whatever. (Not so the marauders of Blackland; but, as already mentioned, in this book, *The Barsac Mission,* Verne, or his editor, shows himself affected by the tendencies of the age, and anyhow these villainesses do not play any active part in the story.)

In only one of his books, *Mrs Branican,* is the 'hero' a heroine, and this is significant of his attitude to women, which is not at all what one would expect; he wanted them to be womanly and to remember that their place was the home. This is made clear in an address he delivered to a girls' school at Amiens.[1]

'Don't plunge too deeply into science', he warned them; 'don't forsake the duties of your sex', which lay beneath the family roof and round the domestic hearth (*le toit familiale et le foyer domestique*) 'A woman does better to inspire verses than to make them', he continued. 'No competitive sports', he urged, 'and no cycling (*pas de bicyclisme*)', and they should never put screeching roller-skates on their little feet!

Jules Verne to warn girls against sport and science, against the delights of cycling and the fun of roller-skates! It sounds incredible, but there we are. It must be remembered however that this occurred last century, and it is conceivable too that he was speaking ironically and hoped that some at least of his auditors would realize this. Certainly in *The Golden Volcano* and *The Barsac Mission*, written some years later, the young heroines are adventurous enough, though their exploits do end in family life within the home.

His closing words are worth quoting:

> 'Now applaud—applaud with all your heart. Not to thank me for what I've said but to express your appreciation—that I've finished!'

With one exception, no heroine appears in Verne's masterpieces of science fiction, and even Graüben, in *Journey to the Centre*, is a very shadowy figure and has to be left behind when the adventures begin. A woman would have been out of place in the balloon *Victoria*, in the space-capsule, in the submarine *Nautilus*, with Captain Hatteras or Captain Len Guy among the ice-floes. A love-interest is dragged quite irrelevantly into *The Begum's Fortune*, and it might have been omitted without loss from *Propeller Island*; it is more appropriate in *The Golden Volcano*, and essential in *A Family without a Name*.

This austerity did not apply to his youthful dramatic efforts, but in them he had been simply sowing his literary wild oats; and though he had a weakness for rather broad jokes, this was only in his family or among friends and they nowhere disfigure his works. As a private individual he might allow himself such things, perhaps as a sort of

[1] *Discours prononcé par Jules Verne à la Distribution des Prix du Lycée des Jeunes Filles*, 29 September 1893.

'safety valve', but he would no more introduce them into his narratives than he would in church. Never did he forget his influence on his young readers. 'If I am not always what I should be', he told an interviewer, 'my characters will be what my best self would like to be.'

Personally courageous, he disliked brutality and violence and never dwelt upon them: where fist-fights, murder, torture, or battles come into his stories he usually deals with them very briefly. Even the heroic last stand of the French Separatists in *A Family Without a Name* is not described as fully as one might expect.

Verne was too patriotic to make any of his French characters villains, though some of them are eccentric beyond all reason. Those who serve as his heroes are less burdened with information, and less fanatically single-minded, than those of the other nationalities; they are courageous, devoted to duty and at the same time debonair. As might be expected, for Verne had had more experience of Frenchmen than of foreigners, they are more like human beings than most of his other heroes.

His villains and other objectionable characters vary in their nationality, but even here Verne never ceases to be objective. Herr Schultz, in *The Begum's Fortune*, an exponent of total war and frightfulness, might well have been a Nazi Gauleiter:

> 'Just think what it would be if I could manage to have a silent projectile; sudden death comes noiselessly, on some calm and serene night, upon a hundred thousand people at once!'

But though Verne makes this scoundrel not only appalling but ludicrous, he pays tribute to his countrymen's virtues by extolling his brilliance as an inventor and by giving him a more-than-Teutonic efficiency as an organizer, dealing single-handed with the complex commercial and financial affairs of a great industrial city!

As was then the tendency among the French, Verne had a great admiration for the Russians, and he managed to reconcile this with his love of freedom by representing the Tsar as benevolent and merciful, always ready to grant an amnesty to political exiles and refugees.

Though Verne has been 'vehemently accused' of being too hard on the Anglo-Saxons,[1] his attitude towards them was strangely am-

[1] J. L. Gaston-Pastre's obituary study in *La Rëvue Hebdomadaire*, 25 February 1928.

bivalent. He scorned the 'Barnum' aspect, and was sardonically amused at some of the vagaries, of the American character, but he did full justice to its enterprise, its audacity, its ability to 'think large'.

His dislike of the English[1] governing and official classes, of what is now called our 'Establishment' was so marked that I am tempted, though, I must admit, without any direct evidence, to suspect some unfortunate personal incident that rankled all his life. On the other hand he honoured the adventurers of our nation, our explorers and seamen.

During much of his career, when relations between France and Britain were strained, he hardly ever looked across the Channel for his heroes. Yet he never forgot that they were there, and among them were 'gallant Lieutenant Davon and his gallant crew' of the Royal Navy, who, in *For the Flag*, 'sacrificed their lives in the cause of humanity'.

Verne's early enthusiasm for science was damped by a growing realization of its possibilities, in unscrupulous hands, for evil. The technicians of the Gun Club seek to reach the moon, again to quote the words of Mallory, 'because it's there', and work openly in the sight of all the world; but later, when they want to move the earth's axis for financial profit, they act in hiding, as callously disregardful of the possible results of their activities as any refugee physicist striving to produce a newer and nastier bomb. They, at their worst, are sane; but Thomas Roch, in *For the Flag*, is insane; and Marcel Camaret, in *The City in the Sahara*, at first merely unbalanced, becomes a raving lunatic—and both for a time obey the behest of a gang of rascals.

As has been seen, he did not agree with the views of Darwin, but it was only the theory of Natural Selection that he rejected, not the general idea of Evolution. His views on this, as expressed in *The Eternal Adam*, might read almost like an anticipation of the modern suggestion that atomic radiations might produce remarkable transformations in living creatures—except that in Verne's story there are no such radiations! Inexplicably, some of the marine plants adapt themselves to life on land; then, as described in a sentence which is cut short abruptly:

[1] Not the 'British'. Verne admired the Scots and the Irish, and never seems to have heard of the Welsh!

'Along the watercourse we can see the former marine animals, mostly molluscs and crustaceans, in process of becoming terrestrial. The air is furrowed by flying-fish, birds rather than fish, their wings having enlarged beyond all reason and their incurved tails allowing them to . . .'

Verne's religious views have given rise to some speculation. His relatives denied the rumour that he, a member of an old Roman Catholic family, had ever turned Protestant, but such denials are not made unless there is something to suggest that the rumour might have a factual basis. It was no doubt due to certain aspects of his work.

There are admittedly a few passages in this which must have made some pious Catholics feel doubtful. Towards the end of *The Village in the Treetops* comes a scene which has been compared to a burlesque, in very bad taste, of an important Papal ceremony. Though in these days of radio and television the idea, mentioned in *Propellor Island,* of listening to a sermon over a wire appears almost old-fashioned, to Verne's contemporaries it must have seemed a startling innovation, and when it comes to making one's confession and hearing Mass by telephone! . . . And surely many of Verne's readers must have wondered how to take it when he makes the local Church authorities decide that the trifling fact that a bride is invisible does not debar her from receiving the sacrament of marriage!

Most of his characters have nothing said about their religious beliefs. Some are described as Roman Catholics, but they never seem to use a rosary or invoke the saints. Some are Protestants—and they do read the Bible. The rascally pedlar in *Hector Servadac* is a Jew by race, but there is no suggestion that he shared his people's faith. Verne was no anti-Semite: the Jewish innkeeper in *Carpathian Castle* is brave and generous.

One omission in his work is almost too big to be noticed, and indeed went unnoticed until a Catholic pamphleteer pointed it out.[1] As soon as attention is drawn to this, one Word is conspicuous by it absence: nobody in any of Verne's narratives, however religious he may be, mentions the Name of Christ. Not the heroic missionary in *Five Weeks in a Balloon,* forgiving the natives who have tortured him to death and dying while at prayer. Not the three space-

[1] M. Moré.

travellers when they realize they are doomed to crash back to earth. Not even the devoted priest in *A Family Without a Name*—who indeed seems to spend more time rousing the patriotic zeal of his congregation than preaching the Gospel.

This strange reticence may simply have been due to Verne's wish to conform to Hetzel's policy of keeping his periodicals free from any sectarian bias while always giving them a sound religious basis. It was in keeping with this policy that in moments of crisis his characters should express their faith, commend themselves to Providence, or return thanks to God. Thus in *Round the Moon*:

> '"Very well! If we die", Barbicane replied with a sort of religious enthusiasm, "the goal of our journey will be magnificently extended. It is His own secret that God will tell us! In the after life, the soul will know without needing mechanical help! It will be identified with the eternal wisdom!"
>
> '"In fact," broke in Michel Ardan, "the whole of the next world may well console us for the loss of that inferior orb called the moon."
>
> 'Barbicane crossed his arms on his breast, saying with a gesture of sublime resignation,
>
> '"The will of heaven be done!"'

Towards the end Verne's attitude mellowed, as is shown by the three narratives each of which might well be regarded as conveying a farewell message to the world. His scientists in *The Eternal Adam* are wise and benevolent, seeking only to transmit the achievements of their age to posterity.

The Barsac Mission suggests that he had even overcome his quarrel with the English aristocracy for Lord Blazon of Glenor is noble not only by title but by character. The hero of *The Survivors of the 'Jonathan'*, an atheist and anarchist—hardly a character likely to appeal to a French Catholic with some experience of politics—is shown as devoting his life to his fellow-men and finally as retiring, as though to the secular equivalent of a monastery, from the world.

Finally Verne's British readers will appreciate the compliment he paid us in what is believed to be the very last of his works. *The Eternal Adam,* written when he must have felt death upon him, shows that he had forgotten his dislike of our 'Establishment' and remembered only the British seamen whom he had always admired and whom he loved to depict. We may well feel complimented that Captain Morris, 'an exceptionally energetic man', and his crew, who rescue the survivors of the world-destroying cataclysm, should be English, so that the last flag which flies above the all-encroaching sea is what Jules Verne had spoken of (in *Second Fatherland*) as 'the red bunting with the Jack in the corner', the emblem of the British Mercantile Marine.

BIBLIOGRAPHY

THE STRANGE JOURNEYS[1]

WORLDS KNOWN AND UNKNOWN

Year	French title	English title
1863.	*Cinq Semaines en Ballon*	*Five weeks in a Balloon.*
1864.	*Voyage au Centre de la Terre*	*Journey to the Centre of the Earth.*
1865.	*De la Terre à la Lune*	*From the Earth to the Moon.*
1866.	*Les Aventures du Capitaine Hatteras:*	*The Adventures of Captain Hatteras:*
	Les Anglais au Pole Nord	I. *(The English) at the North Pole.*
	Le Désent du Glace	II. *The Wilderness of Ice.*
1868.	*Les Enfants du Capitaine Grant*	*The Children of Captain Grant:*
		I. *The Mysterious Document.*
		II. *On the Track.*
		III. *Among the Cannibals.*
1870.	*Autour de la Lune*	*Round the Moon.*
	Vingt Mille Lieues sous les Mers	*Twenty Thousand Leagues Under the Sea.*
1871.	*Une Ville flottante*	*A Floating City.*
1872.	*Aventures de trois Russes et trois Anglais dans l'Afrique australe*	*Measuring a Meridian.*
1873.	*Le Tour du Monde en quatre-vingts jours*	*Around the World in Eighty Days.*
	Le Pays des Fourrures	*The Fur Country.*
1874.	*Le Docteur Ox*	*Dr Ox.*
1875.	*L'Ile Mystérieuse:*	*The Mysterious Island:*
	Les Naufragés de l'Air	I. *Dropped from the Clouds.*

[1] The English titles are those of the more recent edition, notably the Fitzroy Edition.

	L'Abandonné	II. *Abandoned.*
	Le Sécret de L'Isle	III. *The Secret of the Island.*
	Le Chancellor	*The Chancellor.*
1876.	*Michel Strogoff*	*Michael Strogoff.*
1877.	*Les Indes Noires*	*Black Diamonds.*
1877.	*Hector Servadac*	*Hector Servadac.*
1878.	*Un Capitaine de quinze ans*	*Dick Sands the Boy Captain.*
1879.	*Les cinq cents millions de la Begum*	*The Begum's Fortune.*
	Les Tribulations d'un Chinois en Chine	*The Tribulations of a Chinese Gentleman.*
1880.	*Le Maison à vapeur*	*The Steam House:*
		I. *The Demon of Cawnpore.*
		II. *Tigers and Traitors.*
1881.	*La Jangada*	I. *The Giant Raft.*
		II. *The Cryptogram.*
1882.	*L'Ecole des Robinsons*	*The School for Crusoes.*
	Le Rayon Vert	*The Green Ray.*
1883.	*Kéreban le Tétu*	*Keraban the Inflexible:*
		I. *The Captain of the Guidara.*
		II. *Scarpente the Spy.*
1884.	*L'Etoile du Sud*	*The Southern Star Mystery.*
	L'Archipel en Feu	*The Archipelago on Fire.*
1885.	*Mathias Sandorf*	*Mathias Sandorf.*
	L'Epave du Cynthia (in collaboration with A. Laurie)	*Salvage from the 'Cynthia'.*
1886.	*Robur le Conquérant*	*The Clipper of the Clouds.*
	Un Billet de Loterie	*The Lottery Ticket.*
1887.	*Nord contre Sud*	*North against South:*
		I. *Burbank the Northerner.*
		II. *Texar the Southerner.*
	Le Chemin de France	*The Flight to France.*
1888.	*Deux ans de vacances*	*Two Years' Holiday:*
		I. *Adrift in the Pacific.*
		II. *Second Year Ashore.*
1889.	*Sens dessus dessous*	*The Purchase of the North Pole.*
	Famille sans nom	*A Family without a Name.*

1890.	*César Cascabel*	*César Cascabel.*
1891.	*Mistress Branican*	*Mrs Branican.*
1892.	*Le Château des Carpathes*	*Carpathian Castle.*
1893.	*Claudius Bombarnac*	*Claudius Bombarnac.*
	P'tit Bonhomme	*Foundling Mick.*
1894.	*Mirifiques Aventures de Maître Antifer*	*Captain Antifer.*
1895.	*L'Ile a hélice*	*Propeller Island.*
1896.	*Face au drapeau*	*For the Flag.*
	Clovis Dardenter	*Clovis Dardentor.*
1897.	*Le Sphinx des glacés*	*The Mystery of Arthur Gordon Pym.*
1898.	*Le Superbe Orénoque*	—
1899.	*Le Testament d'un Excentrique*	*The Will of an Eccentric.*
1900.	*Second Patrie*	*Second Fatherland:* I. *Their Island Home.* II. *The Castaways of the 'Flag'.*
1901.	*Le Village Aérien.*	*The Village in the Treetops.*
	Les Histoires de Jean-Marie Cabidoulin (le Serpent de Mer)	
1902.	*Les Frères Kip*	—
1903.	*Bourses de voyage*	—
1904.	*Maître du Monde*	*Master of the World.*
	Un Drame en Livonie	—
1905.	*L'Invasion de la mer*	—
	Le Phare du bout du Monde	*The Lighthouse at the End of the World.*

The following titles belong to the series and were published posthumously between 1906 and 1920:

1906.	*Le Volcan d'or*	*The Golden Volcano.*
1907.	*L'Agence Thompson and Co.*	*The Thompson Travel Agency.*
1908.	*La Chasse au Météore*	*The Chase of the Golden Meteor.*

Year	French title	English title
1908.	*Le Pilote du Danube*	—
1909.	*Les Naufragés du 'Jonathan'*	*The Survivors of the 'Jonathan'.*
1910.	*Le Sécret de Wilhelm Storitz*	*The Secret of Wilhelm Storitz.*
1910.	*Hier et Demain* (short stories) Contains *La Famille Raton; M. Re-dieze et Mlle Mi-bémol; Le destinée de Jean Morénas; Le Humbug; Au XXIXme Siècle: La Journée d'un journaliste americain en 2889; L'Eternal Adam*	*Yesterday and Tomorrow:* Contains *The Fate of Jean Morénas; An Ideal City; Amiens in 2000* A.D.*; Fritt-Flacc; Gil Braltar; In the Twenty-ninth Century: The Day of an American Journalist in 2889* A.D.*; Mr Ray Sharp and Miss Me Flat; The Eternal Adam.*
1920.	*L'Etonnante Aventure de la Mission Barsac*	*The Barsac Mission:* I. *Into the Niger Bend.* II. *The City in the Sahara.*

SHORTER FICTIONAL WORKS

Year	French title	English title
1851.	*Les Premiers Navires de la Marine Mexicane*	*The First Ships of the Mexican Navy.*
	Un Voyage en Ballon. Re-published in 1874 as *Un Drame dans les Airs*	*A Drama in the Air.*
1852.	*Martin Paz*	*Martin Paz.*
	Les Châteaux en Californie, ou Père qui Roule N'Amasse pas Mousse[1]	—
1854.	*Maître Zacharius ou l'Horloger qui a Perdu son Ame*	*Master Zacharius.*
1855.	*Un Hivernage dans les Glaces*	*A Winter Amid the Ice.*
1864.	*Le Comte de Chatelaine: Un Episode de la Révolution.*[1]	—
1865.	*Les Forceurs de Blocus*	*The Blockade Runners.*

[1] In the *Musée des Familles;* not published in book form.

Year	French	English
1886. 1879.	*Fritt-Flacc* (with *Un Billet de Loterie*)	*Fritt-Flacc.*[1]
1887.	*Gil Braltar* (with *Le Chemin de France*)	*Gil Graltar.*[1]
1889.	*La Journée d'un Journaliste Américain on 2889* (included in *Hier et Demain*)	*The Day of an American Journalist in 2889* (in the American journal *The Forum*).[1]

GEOGRAPHICAL WORKS

Year	French	English
1867–68.	*Geographie illustreé de la France* (in collaboration with Lavallée)	—
1870.	*De Paris au Rhin* (extracted from the above)	—
1878–80.	*La Découverte de la Terre*	*Celebrated Travels and Travellers: The Exploration of the World.*
1883.	*La Découverte de l'Amérique: Christophe Columb* (extracted from the above)	—

'DOCUMENTARY'

Year	French	English
1879.	*Les Mutins du 'Bounty'* (included with *Les Cinq Cent Millions de la Begum*)	*The Mutineers of the 'Bounty'.*

ARTICLES

1863. A Propos du Géant (*Musée des Familles*).
1864. Edgard A. Poe et ses Oeuvres (*Musée des Familles*).
1875. Amiens en l'an 2000[1] (*Mémoires de l'Académie d'Amiens*).
1881. Dix Heures en Chasse[1] (*Mémoires de l'Académie d'Amiens*).

[1] Included in *Yesterday and Tomorrow.*
[2] Translations included in *Yesterday and Tomorrow.*

PLAYS AND LIBRETTI

The d'Ennery versions of *Around the World* and *Michel Strogoff* have been translated, almost literally, by C. Clarke and E. Philippe respectively, to secure the copyright. Otherwise none of Verne's dramatic work has so far been translated. Another version of *Around the World* has about as much in common with the original as the film, and the ice-show of the same name.

UNPUBLISHED WORKS

An untitled story.
Journey Through England and Scotland.
Paris in the Twentieth Century.
Twenty-four Minutes in a Balloon.

WORKS DOUBTFULLY ATTRIBUTED TO VERNE

1852. Encore un Navire Aérien (*Musée des Familles*).
1867. *Prodigieuse Déçouverte et ses Incalculable Conséquences sur les Destinées du Monde.* [By X. Nagrien.]
1869. *Un Cauchemar.* [By X. Nagrien.]

IN SPANISH

The Danube Principality; The Redskins of Canada; An Ocean Tragedy; A Mexican Vendetta; A Nightmare; Daries the Corsair; The Chinese Pirate; The Transfixed Heart or The Strange Legacy.

IN RUSSIAN

1874. *Travel through Sky and Stars and Around the World in 1,920 hours.*
1880. *Three Russians and Three Englishmen's Air Travel.*
1882. *A Hundred Thousand Versts through the Sky.*
1889. *Robinson on Shore.*[1]

[1] Possibly based on a story by Mayne Reid.

BIOGRAPHIES AND CRITICISMS OF VERNE AND HIS WORK

FRENCH

(Arranged for convenience in alphabetical order)

ALLOTTE DE LA FUYE, MARGUERITE: *Jules Verne, sa Vie, son Oeuvre,* 1928

ANDREEV, CYRILLE: 'Préface des Oeuvres Complètes in U.R.S.S.' translated in *Europe,* April–May 1955

BARLET, H.: *L'Auteur des Voyages Extraordinaires,* 1909

BRIDENNE, J. J.: 'La Littérature française d'Inspiration', *Scientifique*

CLARETIES, JULES: *Jules Verne,* 1881

CLUZEL, ETIENNE: 'Jules Verne et le Préhistoire', *Bulletin du Bibliophile et de Bibliothécaire,* 1957

—'Un Livre Negligé ou les Incroyables Anticipations de Jules Verne,' *ib.* 1959

—'Les Anticipations de Jules Verne et celles de Marcel Robida', *ib.* 1961

DAY, HEM: *Louise Michel–Jules Verne: De qui est '20,000 lieues sous les Mers'?,* 1959

D'OCAGNE, MAURICE: 'Jules Verne', *Hommes et Choses de Science: Propos Familières,* 1930

ESCAICH, RENE: *Voyage au Monde de Jules Verne.* Préface de Claude Farrère, 1955

FRANK, BERNARD: *Jules Verne et ses Voyages,* 1941

GUERMONPREZ, JEAN H.: 'Une Oeuvre Inconnu de Jules Verne', *Livres de France,* May–June 1955

JACOBSON, A. and ANTONI, A.: *Des Anticipations de Jules Verne aux Realisation d'aujourd'hui,* 1930

LEMIRE, CHARLES: *Jules Verne, 1828–1905. L'Homme. L'Ecrivain. Le Voyageur. Le Citoyen. Son Oeuvre. Sa Memoire. Ses Monuments,* 1908

LIVRES DE FRANCE REVUE LITTERAIRE MENSUELLE: A Special Number devoted to Jules Verne, May–June 1955

MARCUCCI, EDMONDO: *Les Illustrations de 'Voyages Extraordinaires' de Jules Verne,* 1956

MORE, MARCEL: 'Jules Verne et Aristide Briand', *Critique*, April 1959

—'Hazard et Providence chez Jules Verne', *ib.* May 1962

—*Le Très Curieux Jules Verne: Le Problème du Père dans les Voyages Extraordinaires*, 1960

NATTIEZ, J.: *Un Modèle de Jules Verne: L'Acteur Paul Saverna*, 1951

NOZIER: 'Jules Verne et les Fées', *Journal d'Amiens*, 15 October 1906

PARMENIE, A. and BONNIER DE LA CHAPELLE, C.: *Histoire d'un Editeur et de ses Auteurs:* P. J. Hetzel (Stahl) 1953

POIGNANT, R.: 'Jules Verne. Écrivain et Précurseur', *Documents Rassemblés*, 1953

RANSSON, RENE: *Jules Verne que j'ai Connu*, 1937

SUTEUX, JEAN: 'Jules Verne du "Nautilus" à la Securité Sociale, a tout Prévu, Sauf la Fusée', *Science et Vie*, February 1962

TURIELLO, MARIO: *Mélanjues Littèraires*, 1908

VERNE, JULES: *Discours prononcè par Jules Verne à la distribution des Prix du Lycée des Jeunes Filles*, 29 September 1893

GERMAN

POPP, DR MAX: *Julius Verne und sein Work*, 1909

DUTCH

FRANQUINET, E.: *Jules Verne: Zijn persoon en zijn werk*, 1942

ITALIAN

MARCUCCI, EDMONDO: *Giulio Verne et la sua Opera*, 1930

ENGLISH

ALLOTT, KENNETH: *Jules Verne*, 1940

ALLOTTE DE LA FUYE, MARGUERITE: *Jules Verne.* Translated by Erik de Mauny, 1954

BELLOC, MRS MARIE A.: 'Jules Verne at Home', *Strand Magazine*, February 1895

CASTLE, GEOFFREY: Introduction to Collins' Edition of *20,000 Leagues Under the Sea*

EVANS, I. O.: *Introduction to Jules Verne : Master of Science Fiction*, 1956

—Introductions to the volumes in the Fitzroy Edition of Jules Verne

HARWOOD: Introduction to Gollancz Omnibus Edition

WALTZ, GEORGE H.: *Jules Verne: The Biography of an Imagination*, 1943

INDEX